# The Power of Pleasurable Childbirth

# The Power of Pleasurable Childbirth

◆

## Safety, Simplicity, and Satisfaction are all within our reach!

*Laurie A. Morgan*

Writers Club Press

New York  Lincoln  Shanghai

# The Power of Pleasurable Childbirth
## Safety, Simplicity, and Satisfaction are all within our reach!

Writers Club Press
an imprint of iUniverse, Inc.

For information address:
iUniverse, Inc.
2021 Pine Lake Road, Suite 100
Lincoln, NE 68512
www.iuniverse.com

ISBN: 0-595-26546-4

Printed in the United States of America

I would like to give special thanks to Lucinda, April, Dawn, Samantha, Rachel, Kimberly, Naomi, and Tammi, and an extra special thanks to Autumn, for all of your efforts and contributions to help get this book in print.

# Contents

# *Preface*

The birth of a child is undeniably a momentous life event for the entire family, and as such is deserving of critical examination and intense planning. Within these pages, you will find a revolutionary but basic approach to childbirth. *The Power of Pleasurable Childbirth* is the story of one woman's journey that led her to the revelation that childbirth can be, and is actually meant to be a pleasurable experience for all parties involved.

Are obstetricians and midwives childbirth experts? How can they be experts on something they never study? Birth attendants are experts on medical treatment, not childbirth, because they never experience birth the way it proceeds without the interference of their prying eyes, eavesdropping ears and meddling hands.

Guided by Laurie's down to earth exploration of the facts, such dangerous myths are exposed and explained. Parents and their families can find safety and satisfaction in childbirth through simplicity. Rather than claiming to be one more expert to tell you how its done, Laurie's words will inspire you to look within for the perfect guidance that is already there!

# *Introduction*

As a woman, a daughter, and a mother—a person—I feel very strongly that childbirth is something to be approached with reverence for the impact our choices have on the rest of our lives and those of our children. I was very careful and researched my options extensively before my first daughter's birth and thought I'd made the best choices possible for myself, my baby, and our family when I birthed with experienced midwives in a free-standing birth center. Even so, I had a vague sense that something was not quite right with that whole approach.

Then during my second pregnancy, I found out about the little-known option of what is sometimes called "unassisted childbirth," and my second and third daughters were birthed safely and gently without external interference. This is the story of my journey to reclaiming my own birthright and that of my child—the joy of giving birth unhindered.

The impact birth has on the rest of our children's life requires that we as parents take full responsibility for our actions. Many people go about choosing a caregiver during pregnancy with the very intention of relinquishing their parental responsibility of ensuring their child a safe birth. Instead, the entire family will benefit when parents take time to find the information needed to make their own decisions.

Have you ever wished that childbirth could be more enjoyable than most women experience it today? Can you imagine that the mental, emotional, and spiritual components of childbearing might have an important influence on the universally-desired end result of a healthy mother and baby? Would you like to experience or help other women to experience a positive paradigm shift in relation to childbirth, for the betterment of all society? Then *The Power of Pleasurable Childbirth* will move you deeply and revolutionize your entire concept of childbirth.

# 1

## *Angelica's Birth*

I started having regular contractions the night before Angelica was born. They were coming five minutes apart for half an hour, so around midnight I called my mom and a friend of mine, to let them know that the big event might be soon. I was thirteen days past due, so I was really ready. When labor stopped immediately after I hung up the phone, I decided to go to bed. I wasn't having contractions when my husband John got up in the morning, so I let him go to work. Late in the morning, my 22-month-old daughter Christiana and I started the day as usual, getting breakfast and watching a little TV.

Contractions started again, and although they weren't painful, they were definitely strong, so I called John to wrap things up at work and get home as soon as possible. I looked forward to having his loving attention. While waiting, Christiana and I showered and got dressed. That really helped me to loosen up, because I remembered how yucky I had felt after my first child was born, not having had the chance to wash up beforehand. When John got home around 12:30, we relaxed together on the couch. Johnny breathed with me through contractions and gave encouragement. We prayed together and called family for more prayer and emotional support. I ate lunch, brushed my teeth and generally made myself comfortable. I also began getting supplies ready, like plastic sheeting and linens. I even set up the video camera, which in the excitement we ended up forgetting to use.

When contractions got really strong, I made myself a little nest of pillows to lean on at the end of our spare bed, and told John that it was time to call my friend to come. When she arrived about an hour later, I was in the living room, concentrating on opening up and relaxing my pelvic muscles. I had an overwhelming feeling that if I relaxed enough, the baby would come out too fast. My feeling was confirmed every time I stood up, because gravity would cause the downward pressure to increase unbearably.

While my friend set to preparing homemade chicken soup in the kitchen, I went to my bedroom to spend some time alone. Christiana entertained herself and visited off and on throughout this stage of labor, tenderly lavishing hugs and kisses on me. When transition started, I began to have painful contractions, so I had my friend rub my lower back while John occupied Christiana's attention. After a few minutes, I became fearful that I wouldn't be able to handle the intensity of the contractions if this labor continued for as many hours as my first had.

What I didn't realize was that the baby was about to be born, and that the painless contractions I had been experiencing earlier were those hours of labor. My friend expressed her confidence in me, however, helping me to remember that I could regain control of the pain once I started the "pushing phase". After she suggested a few times that it would take the edge off the contractions, I gratefully crawled into the warm bath she prepared. As she vigorously swished water over my belly, labor immediately became bearable and I refocused on my goal—a gentle and painless birth.

A few contractions later, I told my friend that I wanted a break in the intensity of labor, and miraculously, it came. My prayers were answered with a long, contraction-free moment in which I was able to regroup and rest. Soon my body spoke again, now clearly telling me that it was time to push the baby out. My friend wondered aloud how far along I was, so I checked inside and was able to feel the head. A few seconds later, there was a gush as my water broke. While pushing with an irresistible urge, I instinctively turned onto my hands and knees in the tub. An instant later, my friend could see the baby's head, so she called John and Christiana to come into the bathroom, and I savored the feel of the emerging new person's head pressing on my fingers.

John came and cupped the baby's head in his hands, so I relaxed knowing she was safe. With one more contraction and three pushes, Angelica Marie Morgan was born into her father's hands! She was a bit purple, having birthed through the cord that had been around her neck, but after I turned over and she was resting on my tummy, she quickly developed a healthy color. We all felt euphoric. After wrapping mom and baby in a towel, John suddenly remembered the video camera and began taping. When we announced that the baby was a girl, Christiana, who had been standing by quietly, now exclaimed, "Baby sister! Baby sister!"

I was triumphant! "Pop a cork," I said, "I feel like having a party!", as Christiana reached into the tub to gently touch her sister for the first time. Then my friend went to stir the chicken soup, leaving us to have some family time. We had begun making plans to get us out of the tub when Angelica began to root around for her first meal, so I settled back in to nurse my four-minute-old daughter. When she was done, John and my friend helped us out of the tub and dried us off. Still connected to my daughter by her umbilical cord, I walked over and settled us into our family bed. Once there, Angelica and Christiana nursed together.

A few minutes later, I felt another irresistible urge to push, and out came Angelica's placenta into the disposable underpad I had been sitting on. My friend wrapped it and gently set it alongside us. Later, I cut the cord when both babies were contented, having finished nursing. John started making phone calls soon after, while I snuggled with my two little girls.

By that time the delicious smell of chicken soup had spread throughout the house, so we all happily devoured our dinners while recalling and celebrating the day's fantastic events. Christiana and I ended the day by sharing an herbal bath while Angelica acquainted herself with her father. I laughed with my friend over the irony, that she had so carefully prepared the herbs to aid in healing my perineum, and I hadn't even torn. We chose not to disturb Angelica until she was well settled, so it was not until that night that we found out that she weighed 8lbs. 14oz. and a few days later that she measured 23 inches.

You may note that there are a few things missing from this birth story. No one told me when I was in labor. No one checked or recorded my dilation, effacement or station. No one told me when or where to sit up, lie down, eat, drink, or pee. No one screwed wires into my baby's scalp. No one ruptured her membranes. Angelica was not touched by anyone outside of her family as she entered the world. No one shoved a bulb syringe into her tiny newborn nose. She began to breathe in her own time, while still receiving oxygen from her placenta. She was not taken from me to be swaddled and isolated in a plastic warmer with a pacifier in her mouth. She was warmed under a towel by her skin touching mine, and comforted by a warm breast and her mother's milk. Angelica was not exposed to the germ-filled atmosphere of a hospital. In fact, the first other place she rested outside of my arms was on her Father's chest, instead of in an isolette or carseat.

The absence of intervention in my daughter's birth was fully intentional. I believe in birth, and I trust life. Healthy babies come out when they are ready. I know that babies are meant to be born without anyone putting their hands inside their mothers. Cervixes dilate (or not) even when no one knows how dilated they are. Monitoring heart-rates, obsessing over dates, poking with needles, etc. do not make babies healthy or happy. Good genes, adequate maternal nutrition, high quality prenatal care, and education do that. In truth, most interventions cause stress, inhibit nature, and dangerously increase the need for more interventions. Even the relatively interference-free care given by most midwives often crosses nature's boundaries. I was quite blessed to have the help of a friend who was truly trusting and aware of these things despite having been trained in midwifery.

It is shameful when technology meant for life-saving is used when it is completely unnecessary. The subtle, unkind interventions that go unnoticed because they are accepted as necessary are just as inexcusable. The violent suctioning of newborns serves as one good example. It is well documented that mucous is expelled from the lungs during birth, and that the rest will drain gently when the newborn is placed on its mother's tummy. Even when suctioning is necessary, there is still no excuse for treating the newborn roughly. The impact birth has on the rest of our children's lives requires that we as parents take full responsibility for our caregivers' actions. Many people go about choosing their caregiver with the very intention of relinquishing their parental responsibility of ensuring their child a safe birth. Instead, parents should take time to gain the education needed to make their own decisions, and insist that birth attendants honor their wishes. Even if that necessitates questioning caregiver's actions, refusing to allow certain procedures, or actually firing attendants.

You might also think, as a lot of people have, that I was lucky to have only thirty minutes of painful labor. But I know that it wasn't luck. I planned to birth this way from the start. Before I was even pregnant, I prepared myself by reading about, praying for, and believing in the kind of birth I wanted. I learned about the fear/pain cycle, and through prayer, allowed myself to be freed of anxiety about labor pain. Without involuntary muscular opposition brought on by fear, my body was able to work as it should—quickly and painlessly.

I also attribute the speed and ease of my labor to the lack of outside influences. I didn't have internal exams because I believe that this unnatural act causes the pelvic muscles to reflexively tense up, lengthening labor and increasing discomfort. I also know that the signs of labor's stages (dilation for instance) can change radically in a short amount of time. Therefore I believe that when an "expert" assesses where a woman is in labor, and that assessment conflicts with what her body tells her, the news becomes a self fulfilling prophecy, and the woman becomes disheartened and exhausted unnecessarily. This helps explain why women in hospitals often give up on having a "natural" birth. They are having longer, harder labors because of their environment. Anyone who could refuse drugs in that situation deserves a medal!

Women's bodies were made to be able to birth without assistance of any kind. I shudder when I hear glowing accounts of birth that include statements like, "the doctor had to...", or, "my midwife needed to...", because I know that a lot more of those labors were labeled and treated as high risk than truly were. So many women are convinced that their baby's birth would have been a tragedy without intervention that, were women being told the truth, it's statistically impossible for the human race to have survived before the invention of these procedures.

The odds that the majority of American women really aren't physically able to birth the way I did are slim. Of the many reasons why so few actually do, acceptance of status quo, lack of education, and lack of desire are all within our power to change. Therefore it is our duty to do so. I have been incredibly empowered and spiritually moved by my birth experience. Too many families are missing the same opportunity because of the over-acceptance and over-application of intervention in labor and delivery. I hope that the story of my daughter's birth is encouraging to other families, and influences them to seek out the information necessary for them to have the births they want. Don't settle for less!

## History

It was difficult to find the place to start the story of my second daughter's birth. I finally decided to begin when my labor started, but significant choices we made of where and how she would be born were influenced by events as far back in time as my childhood. I've always been an advocate for children's rights. For me this means that I disagree with the general consensus in society that children are "lesser" beings than adults. By "consensus" I refer to laws that are made regarding children as well as individual attitudes. For instance, in my opinion it is wrong for children to have rights refused them by law, according to their age rather than their ability. I have always believed that parents should respectfully guide their children by consent instead of punishing. I felt that it was ideal for mothers to stay at home while their children are young; I cannot see the sense in having children just to have other people raise them. Likewise, I always admired home-schoolers for their involvement in their children's education. I had formed all these attitudes long before I even decided to have children.

Where individual attitudes are concerned with birth and the new-born, I have always been appalled at the widespread lack of respect for the person-hood of babies. Most people involved in a hospital birth, doctors especially, routinely act in total disregard for the child's feelings during labor, delivery and immediately after birth. Many people actually deny the existence of any feeling in the newborn, despite compelling and current research that disproves their opinions, and they treat newborns accordingly. Circumcision as a standard practice for instance, has always struck me as cruel (1). I would come to find later, through extensive research, that it is also medically unnecessary.

As luck (or was it destiny?) would have it, I happened to read Dr. Frederick Leboyer's Birth Without Violence as a teen, and found myself in total agreement with many of his philosophies regarding how babies can and should be birthed gently and carefully. For instance, if it is done at all, monitoring of the fetal heartbeat can be accomplished just as effectively with a fetoscope, instead of rupturing the protective membranes and screwing wires into the baby's scalp. Babies need not, and therefore should not, be slapped or otherwise forced to cry after birth. Babies will begin to breathe on their own if allowed to, do not need to breathe right away if the cord is left intact, and can be massaged gently to stimulate sluggish oxygen flow just as effectively. Lights and voices can be lowered in the birthing environment to compensate for the newborn's sensitivity. Early separation from the mother for the purpose of weighing, warming, and testing etc. is not only unnecessary, but cruel. Weighing can wait, warming of the infant is best done on the mother's own bare skin, and most testing can either wait or be avoided altogether. There are too many important observations in Leboyer's book to adequately recount here. I highly recommend reading it, even to people who do not plan to have children, as Birth Without Violence illuminates many probable connections between popular modern birth practices and today's social ills. While I had no conception of how importantly it touched me at the time, it was this book that was my first, greatest encouragement to birth my future babies gently.

At around the same time, in my Junior year of High school, I began suffering from a mysterious illness. It was during that time that I gained a more intimate, and more accurate, perspective of modern medicine. Previously I had seen doctors and nurses like many Americans do, as wise and benevolent experts on the functioning of the human body. During weekly visits to various specialists at that time, I was subjected to an endless battery of painful tests in a vain attempt to diagnose what was crippling me with fatigue and causing me to come down with every single illness I came in contact with. Dozens of doctors prescribed countless dangerous and clearly (even to a sixteen year old) contraindicated drugs for me, without ever finding the root of my illness. Antibiotics had ceased to have any effect on my various ailments, after years of routine use in the treatment of ear infections and sore throats I'd repeatedly suffered throughout childhood.

That year I was diagnosed with everything from bronchitis, to depression, to Chronic Fatigue Syndrome. The true cause of my illness was never found and eventually I just started to feel better anyway. Years later I would find support for my suspicions that what I had been subjected to was not only pointless, but damaging in Dr. Robert Mendelsohn's books How To Raise A Healthy Child...In Spite Of Your Doctor and Confessions Of A Medical Heretic. This, and other similar experiences—from false and poorly handled brushes with cervical and breast cancer, to a bout of whooping cough which I had previously been fully vaccinated against—had such a strong impact on my life that eventually it was clear to me that babies should be birthed as naturally as possible too (2).

# Pain and preparation for my first birth

I have never questioned the fact that childbirth is a natural, normal function of the female anatomy, but whenever I considered it I did wonder why childbirth is so often painful for so many women. It doesn't make any logical sense for one of the most basic and necessary facets of biology to be painful without cause. Like most folks, I have never been a fan of pain. Even the suggestion of pain—in association with illness or any life event at all—terrified me. When I eventually became pregnant with my first daughter, I imagined that childbirth would be like passing a painful stool, only many times worse. That thought haunted and horrified me. I knew I couldn't handle that kind of pain. Little did I know at the time that the pain most commonly felt in childbirth has far more to do with the work of the uterus's contractions themselves than the actual emergence of the baby's body. But still, I couldn't accept pain in childbirth as being normal and natural.

In preparation for my first daughter's birth, I read as many books and magazines as I could get my hands on. I spoke to nurses and interviewed midwives. I watched videos of actual births. I also found myself recalling conversations I'd had in the past with the chiropractor I'd trusted and borrowed books from for many years, including Birth Without Violence. My husband and I took a course in natural childbirth. I studied the Lamaze method of pain management. I worked on visualizations and directed relaxation as described in the book Mind Over Labor, by Carl Jones. I even read somewhere about distraction techniques to avoid dealing with the pain. In the end though, I just couldn't convince myself that such "tricks" were the only way to escape labor pain. Besides, I didn't want to merely survive natural childbirth by huffing and puffing my way through it. I guess if I had been aware or brave enough to imagine it at the time, I would have said I wanted to enjoy giving birth.

Sadly, my first labor was incredibly painful in more ways than one. I had chosen the route that I thought was "natural" at the time, but upon later reflection was really only drug and doctor free. I had done my misguided "homework" exceptionally well and finally decided to give birth at a highly respected free-standing birth center, where the lay midwives are widely published and internationally recognized for their claim to embrace the same non-interventionist beliefs that I had come to know through extensive research were essential to the healthy, gentle childbirth I desired. These midwives said all the "right" things (and still do today) about the laboring woman staying mobile and getting into the positions that are comfortable for her. By then I knew from reading that this is the best policy, for the safety and comfort of the birthing pair. The midwives explained how unobtrusive they would be, allowing me to eat and drink, listen to music or watch TV as I pleased. They also showed me around the beautifully decorated birthing rooms. Each had its own bathtub, supposedly for laboring in. I knew from reading that water was supposed to be a wonderful pain reliever. One of the two head midwives even knew Frederick Leboyer personally, so I was assured that his philosophies were shared by these women.

# 2

## *My first birth*

Needless to say, I was in for a surprise. Late on the eve of what was to be Christiana's birth, my mother, my husband, and I were met by the apprenticing midwife at the center. Until I went to the birth center that night my mom and I had been genuinely enjoying ourselves, having fun with timing contractions, talking, and laughing a lot. Now, it was late at night, and after the apprentice checked me vaginally and consulted with the other midwives over the phone, I was told to get some sleep like a little child at a strangers house, and left in a dark room with the promise that the excruciating pain I was already experiencing was only going to get worse. We all retired to separate beds except for my husband who promptly fell asleep, so I had no one to comfort me. I didn't feel at all welcome to walk about, eat, listen to music or watch T.V. like they had said I could, because every one but me was sleeping. Bless my mom, who tells me now that she wishes she had known so she could have stayed up with me. But at the time I wasn't at all aware of my rights and no one took the initiative to encourage me.

So, I lay awake. Flat on my back in the dark, focusing on the pain, imagining the worst, and I got it. Despite the wonderful fact that my precious baby was about to be born, I was very depressed. No matter what the measurements said about my readiness, I was already having a terrible time dealing with the contractions—a fact which the apprentice dismissed—so the "diagnosis" that I wasn't anywhere near to giving birth was incredibly hurtful and discouraging. For someone who's imagined fears had always been their worst enemy like me, this was the absolute worst thing that could have happened. I ended up enduring ten more hours of labor after that, a good deal of which consisted of contractions that literally peaked for an entire ten minutes, with no rest in between. I really did think I was going to die and I screamed so for hours.

But that dire prediction was to be only the first abuse those midwives perpetrated upon me that night and the following day. After months of hearing from them that first births are without exception longer, later, harder etc., and that the midwives were in control of my progress (they could be merciful and strip my membranes, or prescribe some evening primrose oil, or allow me to take castor oil, but only when they saw fit), I was already feeling totally powerless and accepting of whatever those women said. For example, instead of finding my own comfortable position to labor in, I meekly asked them what I should do, and they were happy to tell me. "Walk now." they said. Even when I was too exhausted to walk. "Sit here." Even when I wanted desperately just to stand still. "Don't make that sound." Even when screaming at the top of my lungs, "Oh my God I'm gonna die!!!" was the only thing that felt remotely good. They insisted on regularly probing me vaginally, just to give me the grim prognosis that judging from their superior experience of the measurements, I couldn't possibly be anywhere near about to give birth. I feel sure now that, subconsciously, I was waiting to give birth until I had the approval of the midwives that I had labored long enough. I was that convinced that they couldn't be wrong.

"Get out of the tub so we can check you." they said, when the warm water was the only thing that took the edge off those horrendous contractions. They told me I had a "stubborn" cervical lip (the entrance of my womb would not fully open—what a surprise!) that they insisted on holding back with their hands jammed into my vagina, causing me even more humiliation and outrageous pain. As my daughter's head crowned, the catching midwife bitched that she didn't have enough room, even though we had expressly desired for my husband to help catch. She also ran her finger between my over-stretched clitoris and my baby's crowning head, "to help me stretch." When I balked at this insult she brushed my frantic hands aside, barking, "Don't push my hand away!" while I screamed, "You are burning me so bad!!" Then, after Christiana's body was born, the midwife actually lost her grip. My daughter's newborn head can clearly be seen whipping violently back on the video.

Despite all the reassuring talk of finding a comfortable position that the midwives had spouted during our prenatal appointments, I ended up pushing my baby out while lying on my back for their convenience. They pushed on my abdomen and pulled at the umbilical cord only minutes after the birth too. They convinced me to submit to an injection of pitocin—a dangerous obstetrical drug—despite my begging and pleading that they spare me the shot (I am deathly afraid of needles), never once mentioning my right to refuse or informing me of the potential risks. They also welcomed a visiting midwife (a complete stranger to me) to put her hands inside my body in an unsuccessful attempt to manually extract my placenta. For whatever reason, be it fear of legal repercussion or distrust in my body, they refused to wait more than five minutes for nature to do her work. Not surprisingly, my daughter's perfect placenta came out on it's own a few short seconds after they decided to leave it alone.

That whole procedure caused me to bleed excessively, which they then said required vitamin shots (more needles) and three days bed rest. The bleeding left me so exhausted that I was unable to relax and enjoy my new baby—let alone bond with and care for her—for the entire three days. They also catheterized me before they would allow me to go home, because I was unable to pee on their command, which caused me a mild urinary tract infection a few days post-partum. After all that, I was bullied and duped into enduring another needle, in the form of stitches for a minor perineal tear. Those stitches, whose insertion stole even more time and peace from my daughter's irreplaceable first hours, popped out three days after the birth. Ironically, my poor bottom ended up healing perfectly without them.

All these obvious horrors and too many others to list aside, it turns out that the strangest facet of my whole first birth experience was that I absolutely beamed with joy about having such a "gentle" and "natural" birth for quite a few months afterward. The ordeal was over with, thank God, and I was very proud to have made it through without drugs or an emergency hospital transport. I still had absolutely no idea that a better way even existed, and I wouldn't find out until later how common this behavior of praising my rapist as a savior really is.

## The innocent perspective of Christiana's birth

To lend a bit of crucial perspective to my bizarre attitude in hindsight, it's interesting to read the version of Christiana's birth as written by my mother, who attended me in labor, just a few days after the event. The following blissfully-innocent narrative was addressed to my dad, brother and sister who were at home in Colorado at the time and written from Christiana's point of view for fun.

---

April 5, 1995

Dear Grandpa Tim, Uncle TJ, and Aunt Brie,

I'll bet you're surprised to be getting a letter from me already! After all, I'm only almost five days old. But here I am. And even though my fingers are really long, they don't quite fit on the computer keys, so I've asked Grandma Annis to type this for me.

On April 1, 1995, at 2:22 p.m., I came to live with Mom and Dad. You would have been proud of them, especially Mom. This giving birth thing is a hard job, but Mom did great, and Dad helped her a lot. She'll never be able to claim she's a wimp again. She began having pretty regular contractions around noon on Friday, March 31, after her visit to the Birth Center. Our midwife, R., "stripped her membranes"—which is a way of encouraging contractions. They were beginning to get concerned that I was staying inside too long. For one thing, I was getting bigger, and Mom is so little, and for another, after the due date, my placenta was already beginning to get tired and not work as well to keep me safe, so they wanted me to come out and see them.

Mom, especially, wanted to meet me. I mean, she already felt like she knew me, after all those months of me kicking her in the ribs and poking my fingers into her, but she was really excited to see what I looked like, and find out my name. As you know, if I had been a boy, my name would have been John Preston Morgan, III, but I wasn't, and my name is really Christiana Noel Morgan—pretty neat, huh?

Well, anyway, on Friday, Mom and Grandma Annis decided to spend the afternoon walking around; that's supposed to help the contractions, too, and it did. They had lunch at Chi Chi's, a Mexican Restaurant (they say it's not as good as Manuel's in Arizona, but it was okay), then went to some stores to browse. They found a neat store with miles of designer suits for lower prices (like Armani $1000 suits for $250!) that Mom wants to take Dad to one of these days.

He's been needing a new suit, since the only one he has is the one he wore to their wedding, and he really likes to get dressed up for work. Grandma Annis says he always looks really "spiffy" when he goes to work, but I haven't seen him like that yet. He's been staying comfortably casual while he's staying home with us this week. Poor Dad—he had a tummy ache yesterday! I hope he's feeling better today!

Then Mom and Grandma Annis went to Bed, Bath & More and looked at household things—lots of pretty sheets and towels and stuff. They had planned to go to Kmart next, but Mom was really tired, so they went Border's Bookstore and got brownies and latte at the espresso bar, and sat and played checkers for about an hour. Mom couldn't remember ever playing checkers before, but she won both games. I don't think Grandma "let" her win, either; maybe it was beginner's luck, or maybe Grandma is just a crummy checker player. Anyway, all that time, the contractions kept coming, and that was new.

Mom had been having contractions for 3 or 4 months (they're called Braxton-Hicks, and they're sort of practice for the real thing), and she could tell that these were different. She told Grandma that she felt like I was about to fall out. Grandma said, "Oh, that would be nice—instead of going through all that labor," but of course, I didn't fall out. After the checkers, Mom and Grandma Annis came home. Dad called to say he wanted to go play darts with some buddies for a while after work, and wanted to know if we could do without him for a couple of hours. Mom told him about the contractions, and he started getting excited. She also told him to go play, and so he did.

He came by with a friend to change clothes first. By then, Mom had asked Grandma Annis to keep track of the contractions, and they were coming five minutes apart. They could tell there was lots of time, though, because the contractions were really short. It takes loooong contractions to get the cervix open and push the baby out, so this was just the early stages of labor.

So Dad left for a while, and Mom and Grandma watched TV and timed contractions. Dad needed to get his hair cut, because on Saturday, he was supposed to go to the Air Force Base for his Guard weekend and he thought he was looking scruffy. Grandma liked his long curly hair, but she could see how the Air Force might not like it (not that it was all that long, just getting a little shaggy). Anyway, Dad's Uncle Chuck's partner Charlotte cuts his hair for him, so about 9:00 p.m. we headed out to their house. It's a long ways away, down by the Birth Center, so we took along all the stuff, just in case—Mom's duffel bag, the camcorder and camera, and all my baby stuff. They were hoping that I'd come soon enough that they wouldn't have time to come back home in between.

The roads here are really bumpy (of course, what do I know? These are the only roads I've ever felt, and from inside Mom, everything felt smooth.), and Mom felt like I was getting bumped out as we were driving down to Chuck and Charlotte's. While Dad was getting his hair cut, Mom and Grandma timed contractions, and played with Madison, who is about 8 months old. She looks awfully big to me—especially right now (I got to meet her when I was only about 5 hours old!). Then Mom decided to call the midwife to ask if we should come home for the night.

R. told her to come to the Birth Center and L. would meet us there and check us out and decide what we should do, so at about 10:30, we met L. and she said, "Okay, yes, this is early labor. I'm just going to put you to bed here (Mom and Dad in the birth-room double bed, and Grandma on the futon in the next room), and we'll keep an eye on you, and pretty soon, I think we'll have a baby." Dad and Grandma Annis went off to sleep, so they could get rested up for later, and Mom and I went to work. I was really ready to come out, and Mom was ready to meet me. About 4 a.m., Mom felt sick, and barfed. I guess that's normal, when you go into active labor (anyway, that's when L. wrote down the start of active labor on our chart).

The contractions were getting harder and Dad woke up to rub Mom's feet. It was pretty funny when he fell back to sleep in the middle of rubbing. Then they made Mom a nice tub of warm water and she sat in there for a while, with Dad sloshing warm water over us with each contraction. After a while, Mom got up and walked around some, and about 6:30, Grandma Annis woke up and came in to help. Mom got back in the tub, and Dad slept while Grandma sloshed. R. had come by that time, too, and I think L. went to take a nap.

Mom was doing a good job. The midwives had taught her some relaxation techniques that involved chanting and motions, and they really seemed to help. The contractions hurt, but Mom was able to breathe through them okay. I was really proud of her. Later, Mom and Dad lay in the bed together (Dad's snoring really helped Mom relax, I think. He felt funny about sleeping while Mom was working so hard, but I think his being so relaxed helped anyway.) and Mom's body kept up its work.

About noon, the stage called "transition" came. I think that means that the cervix is fully dilated (as open as it's going to get), and then the uterus starts to really push the baby out. The nature of the work changes then, and it's supposed to take about two more hours of labor from that point. So Mom was pretty much on schedule, since I was born at 2:22. I'm glad they didn't tell Mom at noon that it would be two more hours, because she already thought she couldn't make it any longer. A couple of times she said she couldn't do it, and R. said, "You're doing it," and she was. She was doing great! I was getting closer and closer to coming out.

I should tell you about the other people who where there, too. About 7:00, Mom's friend B. came. She was the teacher of Mom and Dad's birth class, and then they got to be friends. She's apprenticing to be a midwife, so she got to help out a lot. After transition, she was the one who got to "chart"—that means writing down what time everything happened. Like, for example, every once in a while, they would listen for "heart tones," with a little machine that amplified my heartbeat so they could see how I was doing. Each time, I sounded fine, and R. or L. would say, "Happy baby!" and I was.

The other person was C., a professional midwife visiting from Utah for a couple of weeks. She met V. (the other Birth Center midwife, who was out of town) at a conference a while back, and came to Michigan to learn from these women here. Mom decided that she wouldn't want to do a whole birth process with C., though, because she was a little too brittle and assertive. The others were all so calm and gentle, exactly what Mom needed in the hard parts, so encouraging when the contractions got so hard Mom thought she couldn't make it. So anyway, there were essentially 4 midwives, Dad, and Grandma Annis there to help.

Dad did a lot directly for Mom, and Grandma Annis was more of a gofer and camera person. Grandma went to McDonald's for food for herself and Dad three or four times while we were at the Birth Center, and took hours and hours of video that we'll send you as soon as somebody figures out how to copy it to VHS. I guess Mom or Dad knows how to do it, because they did it before, but Grandma can't figure it out yet. The record button on the VCR doesn't seem to do anything. Mom and Dad have been having trouble with that VCR anyhow. Its remote broke and it won't do a lot of things manually; they got a new remote (for $91!!!) but it doesn't work either. Dad is going to call the 800 number and see if he can get it going.

Well, at about 2:00, L. said, "Look! There's the head!" And it was. I was getting ready to come out for sure. They had a little trouble with a "lip" of the cervix that kept slipping back around and pulling me back in, and L. kept reaching in there and pushing it back over my head again. They even had Mom get up and squat so I wouldn't go back so far, hoping to keep the lip out of the way long enough for me to get out. When my head came out far enough, L. had Mom reach down and touch me. She was so happy to feel my hair that she started to cry. Finally, with a few big, hard contractions, out I came, into Mom and Dad's hands.

Dad lifted me up onto Mom's tummy, and R. put a terry cloth receiving blanket over me and a little knit cap on my head to keep me warm. I was purple, but everybody said I was beautiful. I guess purple looks good on a newborn baby! They kept me there for quite a while, while they were waiting for the placenta to come out. Mom had a few contractions and nothing happened, so they started to get concerned. The placenta is supposed to just come out, pretty much by itself, and it wasn't coming out. L. tried tugging on the umbilical cord, which was kind of hard, since it was still hooked onto me.

Dad got worried that they were hurting me, so they went ahead and clamped off the cord a little sooner than they wanted to. At the Birth Center, they like to leave the cord on as long as possible, to make sure that the baby gets all the oxygen she needs from the placenta until she starts to breathe fine on her own, and I was having a little trouble breathing. There was some liquid in my lungs, I guess, and eventually, C. suctioned out about a tablespoon. She used a little gizmo that she stuck down my throat and sucked on the other end. It seemed pretty gross, but it helped me breathe better. Dad thought she was hurting me, and got kinda mad at her, but I guess she knew what she was doing.

Then Dad cut the cord and took me and held me against his soft, hairy chest, where I snuggled up to keep warm while they worked on Mom some more. They had her get up and squat again, a couple of times, for gravity, but the placenta still didn't come out, so they gave her a shot of pitocin to increase the contractions. When that didn't work, L. reached in and got it out. Then they found out why it was so hard. It was really big. They said she had a placenta and a half, as though her body had thought I was twins, and started to make two placentas, so mine was ready to come out, but the other one wasn't.

Then dad gave me back to Mom and R. showed us how to nurse. At the Birth Center, they try to get the baby to nurse within the first hour. They believe that the closeness in the first few minutes and hours is crucial to the baby's happiness, and they must be right, because I sure am happy. Grandma Annis says I'm the calmest, most peaceful, most contented baby she's ever seen. Not that she's seen so many, but she says I'm pretty unusual in her experience. I don't get upset about much of anything, and since I got used to being changed, nothing much makes me cry. At first, I cried when my butt was bare, but now I don't mind that anymore. Mom feeds me when I get hungry, so I don't have anything to cry about in that department. The only other thing that bugs me is that every once in a while I get a little tummy bubble, and I cry a little if that hurts.

Well, let's see, where were we. Oh, yeah, nursing. After a couple of hours, Dad took me out in the living room so R. and C. could give Mom a few stitches for the little tears I made with my head. Grandma Annis held Mom's hand while they made the stitches; they didn't really hurt, but it's weird having a needle go through your flesh. Grandma says you know about that, Grandpa. And R. knew Dad shouldn't be there for that, so she sent him and me out to play in the other room. After that, they wanted Mom to get up and go to the bathroom, but she got really dizzy and nauseous when she tried to sit up, so they waited. They got her to drink some more water and some orange juice, and somewhere in there, a chocolate milkshake, and later she barfed again. I guess all that was normal enough, but at the time, it was a little scary for Grandma and Dad.

By then, it was about bedtime again, and Mom wasn't going to be ready to go home for a while. They wanted her to eat and pee and walk around safely before sending her home. So they bedded everybody down for the night again. Grandma took me for a while, and R. showed her how to get me to suck on her finger to get my breathing organized (R. said sucking gets the whole body working right), and Grandma fed me a little water (just a teeny bit, since I really preferred to suck on her finger.) Grandma took me in and laid down on the futon with me and we took a nap together after I sucked for a while.

When I woke up, I was HUNGRY, and Grandma could tell because I kept wiggling my head around with my mouth open and snuffling like a little piggy. So she went in and woke up Mom and she fed me. Dad slept through that part. He was really tired. I think he might have been feeling a little under the weather, too, and he did eventually feel pretty sick, on Wednesday, as I mentioned earlier. About 7:00 in the morning, on Sunday, V. arrived.

Now, whereas R., and L. and B. are all very "Zen" sorts of women, very calm, and reassuring, and gentle, V. is very brash and no-nonsense. She breezed in and told Mom it was time to eat, and asked what she wanted. She brought her a bagel with jelly, and Mom ate it. Then she decided it was time for Mom to get out of the bed and go pee—no more of this wimpy lying around! So she started giving orders. She got Mom up on the side of the bed, where she promptly turned green and said, "I'm gonna pass out." So V. said, "Okay, okay. We'll try again in an hour." But Mom was tired of it too, and said, "No, I want to do it now." So they got her up and helped her walk down the hall and pee. That went pretty well, so they started talking about time to go home.

Actually, it wasn't until noon that we actually got on our way. Lots of hugs all around, and then Dad helped Mom walk out to the car and Grandma Annis carried me in the car seat. They got me all buckled in safe and sound, and we headed home. It was almost exactly noon as we were driving away. So we were at the Birth Center longer than usual, because Mom lost some extra blood (oops, forgot to tell you about the liver and B shot V. gave Mom to help her rebuild blood), and was feeling weak. They told her to stay in bed for three days, and to let Grandma take care of things.

We got home fine and tucked Mom into bed, with me beside her. Grandma went to the grocery store and the drugstore to drop off some film and get some food and a few things for Mom, like some bed pads to keep from messing up the sheets, and a "donut" for Mom to sit on in the tub to soak her stitches (she also uses it to sit everywhere, because her little butt is bruised from my arrival).

Grandma's kept busy—holding me while Mom sleeps or takes a shower (because that's when Dad sleeps, too, or helps Mom shower), doing the shopping (yesterday she got me a pillow that looks like an inner-tube so I can sleep more comfortably with Mom and Dad in the waterbed. I put my little butt in the center and the rest keeps me from rolling over where I couldn't breathe. Great invention!), doing the laundry down at the laundro-mat, cooking (on Tuesday, Grandma cooked a real Thanksgiving dinner, to celebrate my arrival, and Mom came out to the living room and sat in the chair to eat for the first time), and generally keeping things straightened up. I think Mom is really glad Grandma could come. I know Grandma is having a wonderful time, helping out and visiting with me and with Mom and Dad! Well, let's see, what else shall I tell you in this long epistle? Grandma is going to keep a copy of this for her "memoirs." I hope you don't mind.

Since I've been home, I've grown a lot. Yesterday, when I went back to the Birth Center for my PKU test (they poked my foot to make me bleed, and I cried!), they weighed me and I had gained 6 ounces. That's another good thing about the Birth Center. Hospital babies usually lose several ounces their first few days, but I gained! V. says the hospital babies lose from anxiety, because of all the rude things they do to them there and for separating them from the mommies. For me, the only time I haven't been with Mom, I've been with Dad or Grandma, and just for a few moments with one of the midwives, and I already knew all of those people from before I came out. I'm just really happy to be here, and I spend most of my time sleeping, eating, and visiting with Mom and Dad and Grandma.

We've had a few other visitors, briefly, too. Chuck and Charlotte and Madison, and Aunt Nan and Gail, came to the Birth Center on Saturday night for a few minutes, and then last night, Grandma Dee and Grandpa Bud came, with Grandma Dee's sister and daughter and son-in-law (Grandma doesn't know their names either, so I'll have to ask Mom later). They only stayed a few minutes. They brought me a huge, old-fashioned baby buggy. It looks like a Volkswagen sitting in the kitchen. Mom and Dad will have to figure out where to keep it—not an easy proposition. Grandma wants me to tell you that if you still want to send me something special, a nice, small, collapsible stroller would be a good thing, and I'll be needing bigger clothes pretty soon. Most people gave me little bitty clothes, which I do need now, of course, but in a couple of months, I won't have anything left to wear.

Grandma Annis and J. made me some receiving blankets out of flannel. They cut it into one-yard squares and then crocheted all around the edges. J. has done it for all 9 of her grandchildren, so she's good at it, but Grandma Annis was a beginner so it took her a long time; in fact, she crocheted one blanket while J. did the other six. They did all that during a weekend in Flagstaff back in March. Well, I think I'm about out of news, and I guess that's good. This will be a fat letter already. Dad feels better today (after his flu day yesterday), and Mom is eating breakfast (don't tell anybody it's 12:50 p.m.; I keep Mom on pretty odd hours, even though I'm not very demanding, they tell me). I'll have Grandma Annis get this in the mail soon, so you don't have to wait any longer to see some pictures. She'll send a lot more as soon as she gets some reprints back.

Love,

Christiana Noel Morgan

# Awakening

I don't remember the exact moment I began to have doubts that my first birth was the most beautiful, most natural thing in the world, but one experience that stands out in my mind is the first time I watched the videotape more than a year later. I was absolutely horrified! I suppose I just needed a whole year before I could finally be far enough away from the overwhelming joy of simply meeting my new daughter to realize how violating it was to have those women be condescending and cruel to me while I labored so hard to push my baby out. Every woman should be so lucky as to have a video recording of such an assault. If there are any doubts about it before, there is no questioning the extreme violation I endured upon viewing the tape. I realize that assault is a strong word, but that is just what touching a woman in a way that makes her scream is. Thankfully, I have since found some healing for this, my first birth experience.

In an effort to creatively approach the feelings of pain and regret this birth evoked and put them behind me, I envision how my first daughter's birth could have been, had I gone back home after John's haircut to labor in my own living room. In the new birth story, my mom and I stay up late, chatting like girls at a slumber party. As we talk I casually settle into a comfortable squat (in my nightgown) on the living room floor and reassure my mom that the birth couldn't possibly be imminent. Before there's time to go anywhere I tell my mom to get some towels and wake up John because the baby's head is coming out and Christiana slithers easily into my hands during the happy commotion.

Baby is put to breast, placenta slips out almost unnoticeably after awhile. The end.

## My second birth preparations/Midwife troubles

I still hadn't fully realized how hurtful the management of that first birth had been by the second time I became pregnant. I also wasn't aware of any acceptable alternatives, so I sought the care of the midwife that had apprenticed at the birth center birth of my first daughter. She had since started her own practice attending homebirths in our neighborhood, and so seemed like the best choice. My efforts to attain a gentle, natural birth for my baby were no less thorough this second time around than the first. At our very first prenatal appointment I presented the midwife with a written birth plan, explaining our wishes in detail. My husband and I both made clear that we were interested in a truly hands-off approach to our birth this time. I was feeling so confident that I would birth quickly that I even expressed doubt that I would need to call the midwife at all, going so far as to inquire about her refund policy, in the case of precipitous labor.

What I didn't know at the time was that this midwife was hiding the fact that her first three deliveries after finishing her apprenticeship at the birth center had all ended up being transferred to the hospital for third stage (placenta delivery) emergencies. Whether intentionally or not, I was being set up to be the fourth. I shudder now, to think how close I came to being her next disaster. I can see clearly in hindsight that she tried to prepare me for such an emergency from the start. I can see now that what originally appeared to be conscientious concern at the time was actually obsessing. The midwife was unwittingly projecting her exaggerated concerns onto my expectations. She even dismissed my concerns when I brought in copies of the book Unassisted Childbirth by Laura Shanley and the magazine Midwifery Today, both with sections highlighted on the subject of placenta delivery. What should have served as a warning of things to come, I brushed off as common birth attendant concern.

I tried to convince her of what I had read anyway; that I could literally wait days for my placenta to deliver, and as long as I wasn't sick or bleeding to death, waiting wouldn't hurt. She had no explanation for the conflict between her approach and the facts, but continued to insist that if my placenta took any longer than an hour to come out, she would panic. The reason, in her words, was that I had "hemorrhaged" the last time. I tried to tell her that my research had shown that the very thing she had done to me that first time ("traction" on the cord) was what would cause a woman to hemorrhage. She wouldn't listen, but now I know that the best policy is to ignore your placenta unless you feel unwell. Let it come in its own time and don't panic if it doesn't come in some predetermined amount of time. Otherwise it probably will get stuck as a result of your fear and tension.

In every other way though, the midwife appeared fully supportive and respectful of our wishes over the next eight months, so we stuck with her. The placenta issue seemed a minor difference of opinion, considering that she was the professional birth attendant. Throughout that time, I was still under the impression that I needed assistance to give birth, despite a growing suspicion that I really ought to birth my baby alone. I didn't know why, but whenever I envisioned laboring I was overwhelmed by a desire for privacy. I sincerely longed to be free to make love to my husband, or quietly and confidently push my baby into the world in solitude. It troubled me that I couldn't envision a midwife being even a trivial part of the birth without feeling tense and protective, but I still didn't think I had any other option.

## An inspiration to birth unassisted

One day while I was pregnant I happened to read a lovely birth story on the internet told by a woman who regretted having anyone at all attend her breech birth. The woman, named Jessica, told of how the midwives' fear of breech birth influenced her to comply with some unreasonable and harmful wishes. They talked her out of the bath, and onto the bed. Out of a squatting position (that was working so well the water bag bulged out and her baby James started moving down in only a few pushes) onto her slightly inclined back on the bed. It consequently took an hour of pushes in, "that silly position" for James to be born. When her water bag stayed still bulging intact during her labor the midwives asked and she said yes to them breaking it, which she described as, "really resented later as well." After James was born someone had already put a hat on him before Jessica was altogether "there," which also bugged her later.

I was most touched by her words, "So, aside from the midwife interference, this was really a wonderful birth. I think anyone is full of shit who says birth is complicated. It doesn't have to be, although I feel for any woman who didn't have a good birthing experience. I know I don't need anyone present at my next birth, from what this birth has taught me. Any medical 'professional' would have determined my birth to be outrageously risky, with a live birth only the result of an emergency cesarean. James was breech, a fairly big baby, and (this I suspected two weeks later) was born with a serious congenital heart defect. His birth was unexceptionally natural and fantastic, and intuition caught the heart defect just in time."

I was very inspired.

# 3

## *Firing the midwife*

The day before I actually fired her, I called the midwife to try to resolve our differences that had, by this late time in my pregnancy become much clearer. In a fit of desperation to secure our business, she went so far as to lie. She tried to convince me with medical lingo that, instead of mismanagement of the third stage I had actually suffered what is called a "partially accreted" placenta with my first daughter, and that I was therefore more likely to require assistance this next time. She could tell, perhaps better than myself at the time, that I was gaining courage and strength enough to birth this baby the way I knew all along that I should. Luckily, I was able to quickly find reassurance that an accreta is actually a rare condition. According to the medical manuals, accreta is an "obstetrical disaster" that requires hysterectomy in most cases (which I very obviously did not have).

She also insisted—perhaps more reasonably—that I would surely need to be reminded to pee, poop, eat and drink during labor. I told her I would remember myself, and she countered that most women forget in the heat of the moment. Her error lay, not so much in the facts of her statement, but in her disbelief that someone could have enough self-awareness to choose to behave differently than "most women" in advance of labor. I have since realized that women who rely on themselves instead of an outsider in all facets of pregnancy and birth are much more in tune with their own needs. I had no idea what a giant blessing the midwife's apparent insanity really was at the time. At first she tried to resolve the whole matter by suggesting that I compose and sign a document claiming full responsibility for our birth choices.

Thankfully, I realized soon enough that, though a signed paper might influence her legally, it could not keep her from bringing destructive attitudes to my birth. And so, the week before my "due date" I fired her.

On the surface, it was tempting to consider this whole experience an unfortunate exception to the rule, but my later research of other women's birth stories would prove otherwise. The only difference I see now, between myself and millions of other women, is that I have slowly come to accept the mistakes I allowed the midwives from the Birth Center to make, instead of glorifying them as necessities. I was then able to take the required, though sometimes unpleasant, measures to ensure that my next births were not hindered in becoming the best they could possibly be. If I had known during my first pregnancy that I need not give up my power and responsibility to anyone else, I could have done far more effective preparation to be my own best attendant. Empowered by this knowledge I could have avoided all the fear induced pain and complications I endured.

## The beginning of a new perspective on midwifery

This same midwife I fired had once claimed to have complete faith in women's ability to give birth. This common declaration is one of the things that midwives are known for, but such a statement is only empty lip-service if birth attendants don't also trust women's ability to know their own abilities and limitations. Most midwives profess to be against intervention, but when it comes down to it, they want clients to lie a certain way so they can see, stop what they're doing so they can check how far the woman has progressed, let them say when to push, and on and on.

There are many reasons for this contradictory behavior, ranging from legal burdens to plain arrogance, depending upon the individual midwife. It's a shame that midwives often act differently than they proclaim to believe, and it's also unnecessary. As I delved deeper into the homebirth community with the help of the internet, I would find that a lot of gentle birth advocates mistakenly put midwives on a pedestal purely because their reputation is so much better than Obstetricians'. The truth is that they are human like the rest of us, and as such are not above scrutiny. But in this world where childbirth regularly suffers tremendous abuses, midwifery escapes much valuable criticism by its proponents. After my two seriously negative experiences, I was not surprisingly convinced that there is much more to having the best possible birth than simply finding a friendly, well-trained midwife.

A burning building is a real example of an emergency situation in which expert management is often truly helpful. In modern society, healthy labor and delivery is seen by almost everyone as an illness that needs fixing by such an expert. Midwives are not beyond such mistaken beliefs. In fact, the average midwife's training in the management of complications becomes all but impossible to forget, if not the entire focus of their work. The problem with this perspective is that a healthy woman's labor is not an emergency. Because of their extensive training, many midwives truly believe that they know how birth should proceed better than their clients. As a result they are inadvertently inclined to be controlling, even though midwives are known for professing that birth is not an illness. Purely out of fear of being held responsible for a bad outcome, most midwives feel obligated to manipulate birth at least a teeny, tiny bit according to their training.

This is an unavoidable fact of assisted birth, as it would take superhuman effort to give up every single ounce of responsibility for a miracle you are allowed to witness. The trouble begins because women are very vulnerable in the middle of labor. That is not to say that she is weak, but the nature of birth is that the laboring woman opens up to allow another being to pass through her. Something so simple as suggesting to a client that she is not competent enough to know her own needs at such a time can easily disempower or distract her. Besides being a hindrance to the entire birth process—and therefore a danger—this also constitutes a serious breach of trust, which is exactly what most women hope to avoid by choosing the care of a midwife over an O.B in the first place.

After my second daughter's birth, a midwife friend would ask me, "If a woman really wanted to give birth alone, then why would she call a midwife?" At first, I thought, well, maybe she's right. Why would she? Why did I hire a midwife for those few months, for that matter? But then it occurred to me that a woman who wished to birth as nature intended ought to be able to call upon a midwife in order to reassure herself that she had extra help and expertise available for the asking. Then she could feel confident that she was totally prepared and safe for the very purpose of allowing herself to relax enough to birth safely and naturally without interference. The ideal would be for midwives to be references and assistants to mothers, rather than deliverers and manipulators. The sad reality is that there are very few midwives that would actually sit on their hands to "allow" a mere woman to deliver her own baby, let alone encourage her to do so.

## Beginning to learn about pain

Throughout my second pregnancy, and in between hiring and firing that second midwife, I felt even more terrified of painful childbirth than I had been before my first birth. This was not surprising since, by then, I had experienced how really excruciating it could be first-hand. While simultaneously trying to sort things out with the midwife, I decided I needed to prevent a repeat of my first outrageously painful birth and went about researching labor pain even more. I felt almost driven to find real examples of gentle, painless births, as well as "how-to" information. My need to find truly positive role models was intense, but everywhere I had already looked women were screaming and crying and being grossly manipulated in labor. It was during this search that I picked up the book that would have a profound impact on all my future attitudes surrounding birth, Unassisted Childbirth, by Laura Kaplan Shanley. I loved this book immediately.

Laura's words genuinely ministered to the part of me that knew that what I had been through with my first birth was not right. Perhaps more importantly though, Ms. Shanley confirmed for me what had previously only been a nagging suspicion; that pain didn't have to be a part of healthy childbirth. Unassisted Childbirth was probably the first book I read that truly helped me begin to understand that fear in child-birth can be a direct cause of pain when the uterus contracts. I began to see that my extreme fear of pain was the largest reason why I had had a painful birth. It was a vicious cycle, the more I feared, the more I hurt, and the more I hurt, the more I feared, and so on and so on. Laura's words encouraged me to examine the source of my fears and begin to work on releasing them. Until that point I had assumed that my fears were an integral part of my being, and I was allowing my fears to make my whole life miserable.

# 4

## *Birth truths*

The first step of my personal healing journey was finding facts to counter my fears. If pain wasn't really a necessary part of childbirth, then I wanted to find out why it remained so common. I had an idea that if I could just understand the mechanics of painful contractions, I could best determine what I could do about it. One of the most helpful revelations I had involved the common misconception that pain in childbirth is primarily caused by the bulk of the baby's body moving through and out of the birth canal. Even though I'd experienced birth myself, I was still under the impression that birth hurt because babies were "too big" to fit through such a tiny opening as the vagina.

This myth is most popularly believed by men, who accept or promote such erroneous analogies as that "shoving a watermelon down your throat" is akin to the pain of childbirth. Giving birth is also not like pulling your lower lip over the top of your head, or whatever Bill Cosby said. Another source of this misconception is an excuse often given for taking drugs in childbirth, "You would never have a tooth pulled without Novocain would you?" The problem with such a comparison is that tooth extraction and birthing babies have nothing at all in common. There is nothing natural about teeth being pulled forcibly from your head.

Through a reference in Unassisted Childbirth, I also came to read Childbirth Without Fear, by Grantly Dick Read, and through the breastfeeding support group La Leche League, I found The Birth Book, by Bill and Martha Sears. In those texts I zeroed-in on the physical details of the explanations for pain in childbirth. What I found was that, in reality, childbirth pain—except in rare situations like posterior presentation or transverse lie—is experienced in the contracting of the uterus rather than in the stretching of the pelvic tissues under pressure of the baby's head.

In my own layman's terms, what I learned was this: For muscles, like those in your arm, working normally is generally only hard work at worst. But if your arm were to come up against some immovable resistance—like say, a 700 lb. bell bar—your muscles would eventually begin to tire and ache. Like the arm, uterine muscles are perfectly prepared and suited for their intended work. But in childbirth, if the cervix and vagina do not open, the action of the uterine muscles pushing against the cervix and vagina cause the uterus to tire and ache in the same manner as the arm. However, it is not natural for the cervix and vagina to be a barrier, frozen from fear. The normal state of the vagina in labor should be the same as it is during healthy consensual sex. That is to say, lubricated, relaxed, and ready to be entered.

The most discomfort that the actual exiting of the baby's body causes—no matter the size—is usually limited to when the head "crowns", or is pressing right at the entrance of the vagina. For some women, this feeling has been appropriately described as a "ring of fire". However, the burning sensation of crowning—like the satisfying feeling of sexual penetration—is most often a relief rather than something to be feared, especially when compared to a painful labor. It is also more bearably brief in a truly natural, unhindered delivery. What does make childbirth painful for many, many women is tension and fear. While it's true that those two things are rampant in modern society, there's nothing natural about being tense and fearful in labor.

## Fear and its relation to pain

Fear as a response to danger has a purpose. That purpose is to stimulate the "fight or flight" response from the brain. In the "fight or flight" response to fear, the brain sends signals to "nonessential" organs of the body (like the uterus) to shut down, in order to increase the supply of blood (and therefore oxygen) to organs essential to fighting or fleeing, like the heart, brain, legs and arms. When a person is fearful—say, in the wild—they are usually in real danger, and this fight or flight mechanism works perfectly to protect the person. Alternately, when a woman is in labor and she experiences even irrational fear, the result is that her uterus is deprived of oxygen, which results in pain. The uterus of a fearful woman has been said to be literally white from the absence of blood. Together with the unconscious resistance from the cervix and vagina, this creates a situation where pain is almost guaranteed.

The happy news about fear in childbirth is that it is most often either unwarranted, or when the fear is very reasonable, the source is usually unnecessary. In my case, as in many women's cases, my fear was an unwarranted fear that intense pain was an inevitable component of childbirth. Finding out the truth relieved that fear, and I was able to let go of it. Another fear that I harbored without knowing it, was of the very real threat posed by the midwives and the dangerous and painful procedures they insisted upon.

When I eventually removed the threat of interference from a midwife, that fear was eliminated too. The result was the nearly pain-free birth of my second daughter, Angelica Marie Morgan. I confess that through about thirty minutes of my labor with her, I panicked and as a result had about six really painful contractions. This was mostly attributable to unexamined self-doubt left over from my first birth. Unfortunately I had allowed the midwives to convince me that I was not capable of birthing as quickly as I had felt I could. Now I'm quite certain that if I had just been able to relax without any criticism or ridicule for wanting a pleasurable birth, my first birth would have been just as quick and comfortable as my second.

## More birth truths

In short, "giving birth" is essentially allowing a muscle that was made to do the job, to push a compact, moldable baby out of an opening that was made to expand painlessly to allow that very baby to come out. Period. The truth is that the uterus is one of the strongest muscles in the body, and was made specifically for pushing out babies. Nature provides for the mothers comfort by releasing chemicals from the brain that send a message to joints, ligaments and muscles to relax. The skull of the baby is also made flexible. For any woman that is not so seriously disfigured from illness or heredity that every day life is painful and difficult, there is literally nothing physical in the way of giving birth painlessly.

In fact, I have personally come to believe that childbirth is a blessing to women sent straight from God. I mean, in its purest form, birth is the most fantastic orgasm married with a miracle! What more heavenly gift could there be? Since experiencing this for myself, I have also come to know hundreds of other women who view birth this way too. That's not at all to say that women who have painful births have done something wrong or deserve to suffer, nor is labor pain in any way attributable to "original sin", because some women very clearly do not experience it, and if nothing else, they are no less sinners than the rest of us. At the same time, childbirth just doesn't have to be painful. Pain is our body's signal to the mind that something is wrong inside. There were no mistakes when childbirth was created—it works as perfectly as eating, sleeping, and breathing.

Just having more information can make birth less painful all by itself. By exposing myths about childbirth I put my own irrational fears to rest. It follows that the fewer fears a woman has surrounding birth, the less tension she will have when she goes into labor. The less tension she has, the less pain she will feel. Notice that I am not suggesting that pain is only a state of mind; far from it. Many women very clearly do have painful labors, as I did. What I am saying is that the very way we choose to give birth often causes that pain. This information itself has the potential to help women experience birth without any pain—not just feel pain a different way—if only they are able to apply it in their own lives.

# 5

## *How popular birth practices harm*

There are literally millions of reasons why women have pain and complications during childbirth. Some are very widely known, and therefore easily pinpointed and avoided, but there are others that are hidden in a sense. Many of the things that cause problems in childbirth are procedures and actions that are so ingrained in our culture as "normal" birth practices, they get overlooked as a cause by even the keenest of observers. There is a simple way to determine the most likely causes of complications in labor though. Regardless of your faith, one can simply imagine how the creator of life itself might have intended childbirth to flow and unfold, and begin to sense how society's most common birth practices pervert and disrupt the original design.

In that vein, it helps to compare other bodily functions to childbirth in order to picture the way birth is biologically meant to proceed. The closest thing to childbirth that everyone can relate to is a bowel movement. I like to give this analogy: imagine how hard it would be to move your bowels with a team of nurses and a colorectal specialist standing by every time. (An audience that is entirely focused on the event having problems.) What if they insisted on monitoring your poop's progress as it came out? What if they stuck their hands in you every so often to see how far the poop had come and how much your anus had dilated? What if they threatened to cut the poop out of you if you couldn't push it out on their schedule?

You may feel inclined to exclaim, "Yikes!" at such a thought, but that's exactly what is going on in most labor rooms today. There is a criminally large number of women suffering constipated labors. Ironically, it is the supreme testimony to the power and reliability of birth itself, that anyone is able to give birth vaginally in such hostile environments as is prevalent in hospitals and even many homebirth delivery rooms. Similarly, women no more need a hospital or midwife to help them give birth than they do to pass stool everyday. Every now and then, someone has trouble pooping like every other bodily function, so they go to the doctor then. But until such a time, everyone assumes that they won't have any trouble pooping, day in and day out. Birth would be most wisely and safely approached the very same way.

One of the most influential and easily changed factors that hinder women from experiencing pain and complication free birth is an ill-made choice of birthing place. Let me not mince words; there is nothing natural about giving birth in a hospital. Women birthing in hospitals are plainly having much more painful births than necessary, for many reasons. But many women feel that hospital birth is safer because there is technology and expertise readily available there. Many who might otherwise wish for a pleasurable birth for themselves are also pressured by guilt into believing a dangerous lie that goes something like, "So long as the mom and baby survive, it shouldn't matter how the baby gets here."

But what if hospitals advertised that they would inject all sorts of dangerous drugs into their patients, hang them upside down, and torture them and their babies throughout labor, but promised a healthy outcome? Would anyone in their right mind volunteer for that? I should hope not. The harsh reality though, is that the average hospital birthing woman goes through almost exactly the same bizarre scenario I just described.

Even without delving into the strong evidence that the drugs that hospitals use to ease labor pain are not safe, I can prove my point. Some women won't even take Tylenol for a headache during pregnancy and fearfully abstain from a morning cup of coffee but will demand narcotics at the onset of labor. Such hypocrisy is ridiculous, but that controversy is only the beginning. The very positions that most birth attendants require women to labor and birth in are indisputably the absolute worst for a healthy baby/Mom outcome—second only to hanging upside down.

Laboring on your back—whether flat or reclining with knees supported—literally closes the pelvic opening, jamming the pointy bone at the base of the mothers' spine into the fetal skull. No matter what the benefits to the birth attendant, this standard "lithotomy" position definitely reverses the benefits of gravity completely, so that not only is the woman's body pushing her baby without the help of gravity, but against it. It doesn't take a rocket scientist to see why it's harmful to physically prevent a baby from being born this way, even though modern women run to birth attendants who require such insanity in droves because we are supposedly unable to let our babies come out on their own.

The vaginal exam is another dangerous, sometimes painful, often humiliating always counter-productive, aptly described "torturous" procedure that is required by all hospitals and most professional birth attendants. Not only does this practice have the serious potential to introduce dangerous foreign bacteria into the birth canal, encouraging infection, but vaginal exams also slow down labor for two reasons. The first is psychological. Obviously it is unnatural to have a stranger put their hands inside of you, let alone in public, and let alone when you are doing one of the most special, most personal things in the world: birthing a baby. The second is physical. The only way a baby can come out of the vagina is if it and cervix are 100% relaxed. I can't speak for anyone else, but I can't relax before, during, or after a vaginal exam.

It may not be common knowledge because it is the mainstay of the birth attendant profession, but it's common sense; inhibiting labor is one of the most harmful things you can do to a pregnant mother and her child. Labor is hard work, and artificially extending it will cause the mother to become exhausted rapidly, her baby's heart rate to drop, and everything else goes downhill from there. Fetal distress and maternal exhaustion often end up requiring a C-section, forceps or vacuum extraction or fundal pressure, which all inherently carry their own serious risks. Cesarean section, for instance is major surgery. As with other surgical procedures, C-sections involve a tremendous amount of risk, the more serious of these including, infection, excessive blood loss, reaction to anesthesia, premature birth, and other fetal injury. Alternative responses for a slowed labor such as castor oil ingestion, breast pump nipple stimulation, herbal labor stimulants, and enemas, all carry their own risks too.

Another "torture" method hospitals routinely employ is starvation. They have to make sure that the laboring woman's stomach is empty just in case all their interventions slow down labor, so that when they anesthetize her for surgery, she won't breathe her own vomit. Not all hospitals are restricting food intake anymore, such models are useful for demonstrating the overall pattern. The birth attendant is geared toward emergencies, and in preparation for those emergencies they create their own.

The IV or "hep-lock" is another good example. First, the insertion of a needle interrupts the laboring woman's concentration. Then, she is primed to receive any number of drugs quickly and quietly. In many cases she must even wheel a bag and pole around like a sick person, or is restricted to bed while she labors. At the very least, she will be required to lie down every thirty minutes or so to be monitored by a machine for a while. Walking is one of the best ways to help labor progress well though, so being stuck in bed for any reason adds another log onto the wild fire of labor impeding interventions.

Consider the ride to the hospital while in labor too. Taking a hectic ride is the last thing anyone in their right mind wants to do while they are coping with contractions. I have personally needed to focus inward, concentrate, and get away from distractions, but I certainly didn't want to go for a car ride! The problem with short explanations like these is that there are hundreds of interventions to be had in a typical modern birth. Some of these interventions are directly and obviously dangerous to mom and baby. For instance, the epidural that, if inserted improperly (as is common), can paralyze the mother. While other interventions are more indirectly responsible for either slowing down labor's progress, or making it too fast for the mom to handle, like amniotomy which introduces foreign bacteria directly into the womb, and unnaturally speeds up labor, often forcefully, which understandably often causes fetal distress.

Contrary to popular delusion, women and babies are absolutely not safer having a healthy birth at a hospital. Actually, they are most often in danger and lucky to escape alive. On the other hand, with the proper preparation, a homebirth can not only be safer in and of itself, but it can still be backed up by the same lovely technology. Having a homebirth doesn't have to mean staying home at all costs. It can instead mean having a healthy bodily function occur where you are safest and most comfortable, and only asking for assistance if you need it. It's just like walking, talking, breathing and eating.

## Reliance and responsibility

It is simply irresponsible to rely on a birth attendant who lives and works, say, twenty minutes away from one's home (and, as is the case with most obstetricians, is not guaranteed to be the person available when you go into labor) to deliver one's baby. Professionals supposedly attend birth to act as a "safety net"—to help in the worst case scenario. But what happens when a woman unexpectedly goes into labor completely unassisted, or the baby begins to crown on the way to the hospital?

Many people scoff at the possibility, but it does happen and curiously, what is often considered to be the height of irresponsibility when planned for, is seen as a freakish inevitability at worst when accidental. In reality, it is highly responsible to plan on delivering your own baby yourself, to become educated and comfortable with the "hows" and "whys", and have supplies on hand at home. Even if some parents, educated thusly still end up giving birth with an attendant present, they are at least doing so fully informed about which treatments are lifesaving measures and which should be avoided. A family who goes into labor prepared to handle their own births can ideally have the best of both worlds. Technology can be available to them should they really need it, but waiting unobtrusively down the street. It is when this technology is used routinely that it endangers both mother and child.

It would be unrealistic for me to make a blanket statement about what I would or would not accept in any given emergency situation. In fact, making decisions about individual situations as they come is an important part of my philosophy now. I can say with certainty though, that if I sought out professional care I would insist that every choice about our treatment be as thoroughly explained as possible so that my child's father and I would fully understand the possible consequences of proposed treatments.

I have come to advocate complete parental acceptance of responsibility in birth, and a certain degree of self instruction equips parents to differentiate between necessary and frivolous intervention in emergency situations. I've learned that even apparently minor decisions can have serious implications, so that no decision should be left solely in the hands of a care provider. It is essential to remember that earthly "experts" just don't qualify for the amount of faith so frequently placed upon them by the average modern parent.

It's important to recognize that undertaking such serious matters as conceiving and bearing children aren't wisely left up to chance. One of the ways my husband and I became comfortable with accepting our full responsibility for our birth choices was by becoming well informed about birth, even though we are not formally trained in any way. It took a good bit of sifting through garbage, and the application of common sense to figure out what is physiologically normal, as opposed to the complications and discomforts that are created by the interference of birth professionals, because there just isn't much recorded about truly natural birth anymore. But what we found is that childbirth is a normal, natural process of the body that takes care of itself when allowed to. The basic stages and requirements of childbirth are—contrary to popular belief—completely within the ability of the average person of childbearing age to grasp and act out. In fact, the part of God's spirit that dwells inside each of us is the most important, and most reliable guidance for all pregnant women.

## Appropriate roles for "birth professionals"

Eventually it became clear to me that birth attendants—midwives and medical professionals alike—should morally serve as no more than consultants to non-emergency clients. Birth "professionals" are, after all, human just like the rest of us, but with some specialized training. I personally found that midwives and natural childbirth educators were very helpful as references for information about the normal courses of pregnancy and labor. Most midwives have extensive personal libraries that they lend to clients from. Even in the case that expectant parents insist on attended birth, all professionals should encourage and help their clients prepare for emergency deliveries, since they don't always arrive in time to "do" the delivery no matter how carefully plans are made.

Birth attendants should not wait to change until women begin demanding their rights. When a woman in labor timidly asks, "Is this procedure necessary?" the truthful answer is always "No." There are few true absolutes that apply to every individual. It is unethical misrepresentation then, for any caregiver to presume or pretend to be able to decide for a family the necessity of any intervention. Professional caregivers of all kinds should instead pay heed to the conventional wisdom, "The customer is always right." The consequences of ignoring this cliché can be devastating, because the decisions made about childbirth—medically managed childbirth especially—can last a lifetime or even end it. Morally, those decisions should always be left to the families who will be living with the consequences.

Birth attendants who assert that they "must" do anything to or for their clients are simply accepting more responsibility than is right. From the perspective of an employer, any hesitation on the part of hired caregivers to explain their proposed actions should cause the client to question their caregiver's motives. If a caregiver has legitimate reasons for her suggestions, she should have no trouble convincing parents to follow her recommendations. Any caregiver who is uncomfortable with her client's wishes should politely resign from that client's service. For obvious legal reasons, release forms should be explained more thoroughly to remind parents of their responsibility, and ideally, emergency protocols would be set and agreed upon early on in pregnancy. Sadly, though, most expectant parents today do not prepare for emergencies far enough in advance to be informed enough to make critical decisions about them.

Whenever expectant parents have a desire to be attended in birth, I encourage them to carefully ask themselves why. I learned the hard way that such an important decision should never be based on assumptions. Obviously, it is important to clarify what another person's role would even be, before one can judge if each individual interviewed will fit the bill. Any time that midwives or doctors insist on doing anything their client finds unwelcome, they are overstepping their bounds. If any person you interview to attend you in labor makes statements such as, "I had to do (fill in the blank) to/for a laboring woman." beware. An example might be a midwife who says she will "let" you labor alone, but she must check dilation or fetal heart tones. These interventions will probably sound reasonable in the context that they are presented in, but be sure and consider before you pay for this "service," how invasive and inhibiting having that person insist on doing something unwanted to you while you are laboring would be.

But more importantly, expectant parents should question whether or not to include attendants in their bodily functions at all. I invited a friend to my second daughter's birth because I valued her as an information resource and a comfort. The most important requirement I considered at the time was that she trusted me. She trusted my trust in my body and God. These were essential and necessary attitudes, it's true. There are even a few other radical birth attendants who have that same extraordinary amount of trust. But looking even closer at the supremely intimate series of events that is conception, pregnancy and childbirth, I eventually came to know for certain that I would birth all my future babies alone, with or without my husband—depending on how we feel at the moment—because I now feel confident in myself as my own resource and in God as my comforter.

As I have already alluded to, mere homebirth is not the safest option on its own. Too many potential homebirth attendants have irrational fears surrounding birth that can be harmful to the laboring woman. I have heard stories from women whose family and friends called paramedics and police out of panic when labor progressed to a point that the interfering person was no longer comfortable with. Even when people do not physically endanger the birthing woman, their fears alone can still have a profound affect on the safety of the birth. Through their body language and her intuition, the laboring woman can sense distrust, panic, and unfounded feelings of responsibility coming from anyone around her during her labor, and as I have briefly discussed, fear is the greatest enemy to a laboring woman, because it causes pain and complications.

## Prenatal "care"

Despite "advances" in science that impersonalize even the very act of conception, few people question its appropriately private nature. Likewise, professional prenatal care is, for the average woman, completely unnecessary and often harmful. The most valuable aspects of prenatal care are based on common sense. Procedures that have little or no chance of positively influencing outcomes, like amniocentesis and glucose intolerance tests, simply create dangerous undue stress on the pregnant woman. On the other hand, it's obviously important to have a healthy diet and reduce or avoid smoking, alcohol, and drugs.

Women can make their own decisions about the weight that is healthy for them with information that is readily available too. A pregnant woman can very effectively monitor her baby's well being herself through a natural awareness of its movement too. Sadly, this important communication between mother and unborn child is often downplayed, ignored, or masked by emphasis on less conclusive measurements.

If they are interested women are fully capable of performing most other well being checks themselves, such as measuring fundal growth and checking cervical dilation and effacement. The book Special Delivery, by Rahima Baldwin, explains many of these procedures in detail. If a woman had reason to be concerned, she could check her own blood pressure, maternal and fetal heart rates as well. In fact, readings done by the woman herself when calm and relaxed are more likely to be accurate. The truth is that a large reason so many women are diagnosed with high blood pressure is that monitoring and the environment it is usually done in are stressful themselves. Take away the stress and you take away the high blood pressure (3). In his ground breaking book, Metabolic Toxemia of Late Pregnancy: A Disease of Malnutrition, Dr. Thomas H. Brewer also suggests an important connection between the restrictive "preventive" diets that obstetricians routinely recommend and toxemia.

Of all the elements of standard prenatal care I've found to be unnecessary, I have come to feel very strongly that estimating the weight of the fetus should never be done. Not only are estimates almost always completely wrong—ultrasound, for instance, is said to have a range of inaccuracy two pounds over and two pounds under the estimated weight! What use could it possibly be, to know that your baby could be anywhere from six to ten pounds?—but most especially because even a ten pound baby can have a tiny head and shoulders. Likewise, a six-pound baby can have a large head. Frankly, size estimates are most often frightening with no benefit. It's foolish to focus worry on the unknowable, especially when fear increases the risk of pain and complications. Higher birth weight babies tend to be healthier anyway, and full term births are safest.

The definition of "full term" is completely relative to individual babies though. The estimation of due dates is harmful and inaccurate at best as well. Often, doctors arrogantly disregard a woman's own knowledge of her conception date when calculating a due date. Later, this completely random number is used to justify the use of powerful labor inducing drugs that can lead to many complications including uterine rupture (4) and premature birth. Women's monthly cycles vary naturally and likewise, so do lengths of gestation. Many methods used to calculate due dates are deceptively based on a twenty-eight day cycle. So, if a woman normally goes thirty days from one period to the next, she can generally expect her pregnancy to last longer. The traditional use of a forty-week gestation as a reference is inappropriate, as statistics show that forty-one to forty-two weeks is closer to the average, especially for first births. Just like many other studies that are skewed by routine, but unnatural, birth practices, we must keep in mind that these don't take into account the epidemic of routinely performed inductions.

## Myths and misunderstandings

In order to illustrate the danger of modern birth myths a bit more, it helps to examine the idea that if a baby is born with the cord around its neck that it is somehow in danger. To put it bluntly, all the hype and fear surrounding what is called, "nuchal cord" is just that; hype. This may be surprising to some, but I personally haven't met more than a handful of women whose baby's cord wasn't around its neck at birth. In fact, it is such a common occurrence that if you asked around you might not find anyone who had not experienced it either.

This is not some fatal flaw in the birth process, it's one of many normal and natural occurrences whose risks are routinely exaggerated and exploited. Obstetricians and midwives sometimes use the fear of cord around the neck to convince women that their services are, indeed, as needed as they say. But what contributes most to the irrational fears of the masses, is when birth attendants proudly declare an evil umbilical cord as the culprit necessitating any and every intervention they did up to that point. Once you become aware of the pattern, it is astonishing how often you hear, "We're so glad for the cesarean because—as it turns out—the cord was wound tightly around our baby's neck!"

There is another harmful childbirth myth that says that some women just naturally lose their capacity for reason during childbirth, to the point of being unable to avoid or handle complications. It's true that childbirth requires what would be most accurately described as a "change of consciousness" in the woman. During transition the laboring woman must fully surrender to the power of birth and allow it to overtake her. It can be an empowering spiritual moment where every ounce of her relies on the part of God that resides inside us all, or it can be a frightening moment where she looses all control. Either way it is surrender.

But feeling weak and tired or totally focused inward is a healthy part of transition for some women. Simply knowing that possibility in advance can help individual women decide the proper action to take when she goes into labor. On the other hand, feeling weak and tired can simply be a sign that one needs to eat, drink, lie down, or something else. Listening to your heart is of utmost importance. My personal belief is that God really does reside there in all of us and He won't let us down, but only if we rely on Him.

While reading hundreds of birth stories, I noticed that something funny happens when a woman gives birth unattended. When there is only mom and baby in control, suddenly mom becomes accountable for the outcome. This can happen regardless of how the woman felt about birth before. The reason so many women forget to eat, drink, pee, poop, walk, dance, masturbate, un-loop the umbilical cord, etc. during an attended labor is that they have given up their responsibility for the birth to an outsider. When she is alone however, a woman will find within herself the strength and wisdom to birth her baby just as she needs to. Choosing to birth alone certainly allows one to plan better than doing so accidentally. It is possible to choose to ignore one's own inner wisdom too, which also leads to the many dangers I have outlined so far and more.

To get back to what one can do if a baby is born with its cord around its neck, in most cases you can gently loop the cord over the head with a finger. If not, you can probably push the baby out through the cord. I ended up doing just that with my second daughter. In fact, she came out so fast, there was no time to "do" much of anything even if somebody had been there to "manage" the birth. Such management of birth actually creates emergencies out of normal occurrences like nuchal cord. Interventions such as vaginal exams, unnatural positioning, telling the woman not to push until the doctor gets in the room, and ignoring the natural modesty of the mother, all slow labor down. It is when labor is slowed artificially that the wrapping of the cord becomes potentially problematic. If the cord is tight around the neck for a long period of time then the baby loses oxygen to the brain. So, in my opinion, the proper focus should be on how to make labor as pleasurable, stress free, and uninhibited as possible, not on by whom or how the cord will get unwrapped.

Something else that artificially makes nuchal cord problematic is women's own distrust of their bodies. We are taught to be disconnected from and distrustful of intuition and instinct. But when you speak to women who have had "primal," unhindered births with a complication, you learn that the body knows what to do when there is a problem. Women who experience interference-free birth speak frequently of getting into the physiologically correct position for a malpositioned baby to be born instinctually, or without any foreknowledge of proper "techniques".

My friend Jessica, whose midwives' presence was an intrusion, knew deep in her heart that something was "wrong" with her newborn son even though he appeared completely healthy. She took him to be examined by a doctor, based on this feeling alone and found out that he had a heart condition that was usually fatal and required immediate surgery. But she "knew". If you are trusting and listening to your heart, you will also have the presence of mind to reach down and un-loop the cord, if that is what is needed. It's true that most women when asked today wouldn't know the first thing to do if their baby's cord was around its neck at birth. However, if those same women knew, before-hand, that they would be relying on themselves in labor, they would surely choose to be more appropriately prepared. It is, of course, also wise to learn infant resuscitation. Many hospitals offer free courses on infant CPR.

That brings me to one of the most important reasons why people insist on being attended in birth, and that is the possibility of death. The fact is that death is a possible outcome no matter what environ-ment you choose to birth in, but many people choose unsafe birthing places and companions with the misguided intention of escaping death. To be satisfied and fully responsible for any birth choice how-ever, we must accept that some tragedies are beyond our control. This does not mean though, that we have no say in how a tragedy is man-aged. It is important to consider beforehand, how various choices would impact such situations as a miscarriage or the quality of the short life of a terminally ill baby. For example, I personally would only ever agree to tests that had the potential to uncover a truly "fixable" problem, the treatments for which I was morally comfortable with, and procedures that had the potential to heal. I would not ever abort a fetus. I say this, not to promote my own beliefs, but to demonstrate the fact that the consideration individual needs and preferences are of extreme importance.

My husband and I would accept or rule out individual tests and pro-cedures by becoming as informed of each one individually as possible and carefully weighing the risks against the benefits. If tests we had agreed to proved convincingly that we were in trouble, I might agree to life-saving intervention as I and/or my husband saw the situation requiring at the time. I believe strongly that a child who has no chance of survival deserves to die in the most loving and painless environment possible. We would be careful not to allow painful procedures that had a small chance of changing the outcome to be done to our children, because we believe that it is cruel for a dying person to be subjected to hundreds of painful procedures while isolated from human contact in his last days. In my opinion, it is much more humane to allow life to pass away while the baby enjoys the communication of love through skin on skin contact, nursing, and a continuation of the symbiosis with mother that it knew in the womb.

A pregnant couple should also consider how they would most want to deal with the child's body in the case of a death, before such choices must be made irreversibly. In the hospital, the routine may be for the child's body to remain on the premises to be examined and disposed of rather carelessly. Parents, then, will want to consider if they might want to be able to hold and look at their baby, or even bury him or her in privacy. It's not unusual to be repulsed by such thoughts because our society considers talk of infant death taboo, but tragically, many people are haunted with the grief of never having been able to see, hold and care for their tiny deceased loved ones. For some this makes it difficult to feel closure on their pain. Therefore, this subject should definitely be addressed during pregnancy if not before.

## Sex and birth, pain and complications

The inherent sexual nature of birth quite clearly makes birthing with attendants undesirable. Imagine how a woman feels when she is really turned on and open to being sexually "penetrated". That same feeling of total relaxation and lubrication of the vaginal walls experienced in healthy sex is the absolute most conducive environment to allowing any baby to slide gently and easily into the world. It is quite possible that no woman who actually desires an attended birth can fully fathom the truth of my example, however. I believe this is due, at least in large part, to the widespread sexual abuse endured, especially here in America. Women who have been sexually trespassed once, usually find themselves also raped of the ability to experience total relaxation and pleasure in any sexual act. Consequently, I believe that the sensuality and sexuality of birth has been robbed from almost all women who have not yet healed emotionally from past sexual abuse.

This serves as an explanation for the over-acceptance of medical management of birth as well. Many American women are simply continuing a long cycle of abuse, as is common of many victims. The widely recognized psychological pattern of the abused daughter who grows up and marries a wife beater is a clear example. Many of us do something comparably bizarre by inviting people to violate us in the birth process: the birth attendant. Once a woman is victimized it takes a great revelation or move of God for a woman to take back her own power and not place herself in the victim role again. An interesting example of this phenomenon is the fact, as reported in the book Silent Knife by Nancy Wainer Cohen, that twenty-five percent of women who undergo cesarean section will be sterilized within two months of the birth. This is a shocking statistic, especially when you consider that it neglects to include all the vasectomies that are also performed after a surgical birth.

The trouble is, I don't think I've met a woman yet who hasn't been molested in some way, somehow by the time she reaches her twenties. The fact that we are taught to believe that much of it is all normal and necessary victimizes us even more. When I mention sexual molestation, most people imagine the kind that occurs in many children's homes, but in truth, many of us allow perfect strangers to violate us and our children under the guise of modern medicine every day.

The pattern begins at birth. Americans as a society regularly accept genital mutilation of baby boys in the form of circumcision, or at least forceful retraction of the foreskins of those who remain intact. Both of the sexes are also subjected to anal penetration with thermometers as a routine, and many milder forms of non-consensual manipulation of the infant's body. For many women, molestation moves again into the professional realm around puberty when we are instructed by our own parents to submit to doctors and gynecologists under the guise of "check ups". They scrape around inside our private parts for pap smears, poke around our vaginas and anuses and touch girls' bare chests, all for various "preventative" reasons.

Later in life we surrender dutifully to fittings for birth control devices, and big machines squashing and irradiating our breasts to monitor their health, because so many of us have been discouraged to protect our own breasts and our daughters' through ecological breast-feeding. When viewed with a keen eye, it's all very obviously perverted. There is simply a natural progression from the acceptance of these procedures to the medicalization of the ultimate expression of our sexual selves; conception, pregnancy, labor, and birth.

Regardless of whether a woman experiences her labor as sexual, it is simply inherently so. Nature necessitates that we create children through sex, and babies are birthed through our sex organs. Disassociating one's spirit from the sex act itself, while possible, is not healthy. In fact, denial of the sexual side of birth can very easily cause some women to experience the intense sensations of birth as pain, all by itself. Before the birth of my first daughter, I had rarely been able to experience painless intercourse. My vaginal muscles were just too tight. I was able to orgasm alone, but not with a partner. I knew that my inability to relax was "all in my head" as they say, but was at a loss as to how to change. This was another reason my first birth was so terrifyingly painful and my perineum tore.

## Faith and healing

My own sex life, and therefore my birthing, actually began moving closer to healing when I started seeing a counselor during my first pregnancy. I had been suffering from severe depression for many years, and on a desperate impulse one night, called a hotline that put me in touch with a random mental health practitioner through my husband's health care plan. The whole story of my healing from depression is too long to recount here, but a significant step in my progress to unhindered childbirth came when the counselor asked if I had ever been sexually abused. At the time, I responded truthfully that I was not sure, but explained how I suffered from many of the classic symptoms. She and I didn't explore that particular issue any further together, but somehow, as my emotional life began to heal and I learned trust and faith, the sexual part of me began to heal as well.

About a year later I began attending a charismatic Christian church with my husband on occasion. That is when I began to understand the importance faith has in birth. It was at that church that I happened to pick up the book Supernatural Childbirth by Jackie Mize, and found scriptural references to back up what I was slowly beginning to understand. In her book, Mize said, "Faith is having confidence, being totally at peace—confident that it is all working." Those words were truer than I could ever imagine at the time. Now I know from experience that there is no question as to the safety of a truly faith filled birth.

Some people of the Christian faith rationalize attended birth with all sorts of excuses that boil down to the implication that God can't make all births perfect. The reality is that God doesn't make all births perfect for different reasons in each individual case, but He is nothing if He isn't capable. The truth is that no matter where you choose to birth or who with, the possibility exists that the baby or mother could die or be injured. Most people try to escape this reality by relying on the expertise of human attendants, but this is folly. While God is certainly not our "errand boy," answering our every command to give us the perfect birth, God does want us to believe that He has the best plan for us. He wants us to rely on Him to get us through trials and tragedy and believe that He can use it for good.

What I have learned is that either God is leading me or I am leading me, but when God leads me, I cannot "fail" in any sense of the word. One either has faith in God or doesn't. There's no way to halfway trust God, and when life circumstances require us to have faith, nothing less will do. I don't truly have faith if I am sure that what I want won't happen. James 1:5-8 says, "If any of you lacks wisdom, he should ask God, who gives generously to all without finding fault, and it will be given to him. But when he asks, he must believe and not doubt, because he who doubts is like a wave of the sea, blown and tossed by the wind. That man should not think he will receive anything from the Lord; he is a double minded man, unstable in all he does." I feel in my heart that many who question the safety of birth—God's creation—are, in regards to faith, feeling "blown and tossed by the wind."

We are able to create pain simply by believing in it, and likewise we can create an enjoyable labor through our beliefs. I learned that I have a choice in what I believe about birth and I started to purposely choose to believe it could be pleasurable. The night before I decided that I needed to fire my midwife, God spoke to me very clearly, saying, "Laurie, if you try to control this birth and second guess ME, the birth may be uneventful with a healthy baby/mom outcome, but you will be missing the greatest opportunity in your life so far to give your trust fully to ME and witness with your heart MY full power and trustworthiness. This birth is the key to opening your faith wide and allowing it to succeed to such a degree as to support you for the rest of your life. If you do not stand firm and demand what is right, no matter how difficult that is, NOW at your child's birth, then when? And what is the value of standing up when it is not difficult or important? There is none."

At about the same time, the couple who had raised my husband spiritually as a teen began ministering to me about living in fear. We deliberately prayed together, asking for healing of any experiences of sexual abuse and its symptoms. Along with my willingness to change, counseling, and a great deal of prayer, some of my healing can also be attributed to my husband. Thankfully, John has always been a patient, gentle and generous lover. He trusted me and God, and was always accepting of my desire to lead in the bedroom. He also listened carefully and was not judgmental or angry about my slow progression to sexual health.

# 6

## *Angelica's birth: the blanks filled in*

The night before my second daughter was to be born I started having comfortable but regular contractions. Whereas I'd had strong contractions every thirty minutes or so for the past few weeks, now they came five minutes apart for half an hour, so I called my mom and my girlfriend at around midnight to let them know that the big event might be soon. I was thirteen days past my estimated "due date", so I was really emotionally ready. When labor stopped immediately after I hung up the phone, I decided to go to bed. I wasn't having contractions when my husband John got up in the morning either, so I let him go to work. Late in the morning, my 22-month-old daughter Christiana and I started the day as usual, getting breakfast and watching a little TV. Contractions started again, and although they weren't painful, they were definitely strong, so I called John to wrap things up at work and get home as soon as possible. I looked forward to having his loving attention.

While waiting, Christiana and I showered and got dressed. I was very deliberate about showering and brushing my teeth and hair. Not only was this relaxing and invigorating, it was also a spiritually cleansing and satisfying personal ritual that really helped me to loosen up. This was in stark contrast to the disgust I had felt following my first daughter's birth, not having had the chance to wash up before hand and then being bedridden for three days. I also donned a white embroidered lace nightgown that I had handmade for the occasion of my pregnancy and labor. I had purposefully kept it clean and ready the last two weeks preceding this day

When Johnny got home around 12:30, we relaxed together on the couch. We laughed together as he showed me how students are taught to breathe during exercises in his Martial Arts classes. He breathed with me through contractions and continually encouraged me with loving words and gentle touch. John and I also prayed together and he called faithful family members for more prayer and emotional support. We listened to our favorite inspirational Christian praise music the whole time. Some of the time I rocked in my rocking chair. I sucked on a grape Popsicle. I ate lunch, and generally made myself comfortable. I also began getting supplies ready, like plastic sheeting and linens for the bed. I even set up the video camera, which in the excitement we ended up forgetting to use.

## The video camera

There is actually more to it than just forgetfulness: the reason I never turned the camera on was that the video seemed to be timing my birth. Any time I would remember the camera, I worried, "If I start filming now, what if I am not really as far along as I feel and we run out of film?" The camera was pressure. I know now that it can be difficult enough to find support to surround ourselves with from our own minds and families. Having a camera rolling during this birth would have been like inviting a bunch of people to watch and judge me, who weren't on my wavelength about birth. This first time I was birthing unhindered that would have been threatening.

One of the instances where I began to grasp this concept was in the later review of Christiana's birth center birth. I distinctly "felt" the midwives believing that I had to labor for a certain amount of time before they would admit that I could be having "real" labor. I feel sure now, that I subconsciously extended the length of my labor just to conform to their beliefs that first time labors are long and excruciating.

Labor naturally varies in length from woman to woman, but I now believe that it was never meant to be torturously long. I am not referring to the standard obstetrical viewpoint that if a woman does not deliver within a certain number of hours after labor begins that she should be induced, but that the truly unhindered, biologically normal labor that I advocate, will not exhaust the mother. Laura Shanley once told me, "It just doesn't make sense that birth should take a long time. But fear is pretty powerful and most women are afraid of birth. Hence most women have long labors." I can't agree more.

That said, here are video stills from the first minutes after Angelica's birth. With no one watching a clock, we did not document the exact time of Angelica's birth, so no one even knows how soon after the birth this video was started. We think John picked up the camera as soon as he handed Angelica to me, but we are not sure. I think the joy and pleasure we experienced through her birth is quite evident, even so.

Angelica less than five minutes old.

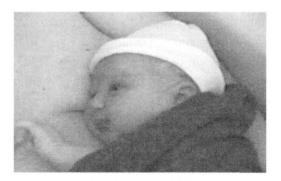

No, babies do not have to cry after birth.
This is most definitely a smile!

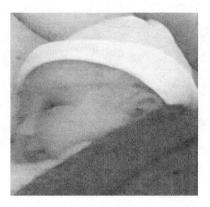

This is how birth should feel!

A triumphant woman!

Yes little one, I love you too!

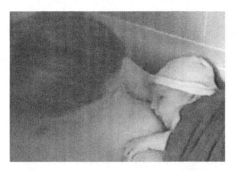

Look Christiana, your sister is nursing!

Welcome to our family bed Angelica.

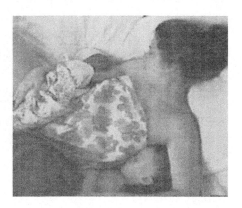

I have never felt so good!

## Privacy matters

John's loving presence was important to my opening up for the baby because by then we were both aware of the sensuality surrounding birth. Creating this child was an intimate act of love between the two of us, and birthing in a loving way simply and naturally completed that act. As a result of healing from past sexual abuse achieved through faith, I was much more able to open up during this labor than I had been during my first. I had become able to make my vagina wet and open by fantasizing about making love to my husband—something I hadn't been able to do before—so I found visualizing having sex during labor naturally helpful.

John and I both welcomed the idea of actually having sex during labor, but I happened to be focused elsewhere at the time. We knew that besides relaxing and bonding the couple, the man's semen naturally ripens the cervix in the same way that the "gel" (which a good friend of mine researched and found out is actually made from PIG sperm!) inserted unceremoniously into the vagina by obstetricians does. In any case, I had enjoyed masturbating frequently in the days preceding this one and found even solo orgasm to be a safe, appropriate, and pleasurable way to encourage strong, productive contractions. Laboring in the environment of my own home was absolutely crucial to accepting and expressing these beneficial feelings.

When contractions got really strong, I made myself a little nest of pillows to lean on at the end of our spare bed, and told John that I wanted him to call my friend to come. When she arrived about an hour later, I was still in the living room, concentrating on opening up and relaxing my pelvic muscles. I had an overwhelming feeling that if I relaxed enough, the baby would come out too fast. That feeling was affirmed every time I stood up, when gravity would cause the downward pressure to increase unbearably.

When my friend arrived she set to preparing homemade chicken soup in the kitchen, so I went to my bedroom to spend some time alone. For some reason it felt incredibly appropriate to crawl the whole way to the bedroom on my hands and knees, and so, as ridiculous as it may seem I did. In the meantime, Christiana entertained herself and visited the bedroom off and on, tenderly lavishing hugs and kisses on me. Despite dire warnings that labor would frighten her from people who didn't understand that she was like a soul mate to me, I actually delighted in cuddling and playing with her.

It's important to clarify here, that inviting a close friend to my birth was just what I needed to do at the time. It was one last vestige of my previous dependency on outsiders for my birthing strength, in a sense. But I have learned a lot the hard way from the experience that I want to pass on. Many people have remarked after reading this birth story in its original form, that having a friend's reassuring presence during labor and birth appears to be a "happy medium" between more interventive midwifery or obstetrical care and the full responsibility of couples birth, but I can't disagree more. Yes, this birth turned out beautifully at the time, but there were a number of significant drawbacks to this one compromise that aren't obvious on the surface. They all surround the fact that birth is a profoundly private, sexual event. Period.

I believe that God made birth and sex amazing and powerful, and usually our bodies overcome the breaches in privacy that are so common today; sometimes gracefully, sometimes not. But just as the physical act of having sex can be done publicly, but truly making love cannot, in order to have a truly uncomplicated, unhindered, pleasurable birth, spectators cannot be involved. Don't get me wrong, at the time my friend was respectful and did her best to blend in with the furniture, but looking back, I can see how even this small intrusion left me feeling like a stranger in my own home.

People today pay a lot of lip service to the idea that women should birth and labor where they are most comfortable. This is good in and of itself, but what most people tend to ignore is the fact that we are never truly comfortable with anyone besides our mates staring at our most private parts and witnessing our bodily functions! All this is to say that I don't plan on ever inviting friends to attend me in labor again in the future, and I highly recommend against it to others. It's pointless to second guess my past now, but next time I will definitely feel free to labor in whatever part of my home I'm truly most comfortable in, and my husband and I will be as intimate as the mood truly strikes us.

## More details

To get back to the story, when transition started I panicked and began to have a few painful contractions, so I had my friend rub my lower back. My loud, angry vocalizations did start to frighten Christiana then, so John kept her entertained with him in the living room. After a few minutes, I became fearful that I wouldn't be able to handle the intensity of the contractions if this labor continued for as many hours as my first had. What I didn't realize was that the baby was about to be born, and that the painless contractions I had been experiencing earlier were those "hours of labor."

I had been so convinced by the midwives who attended Christiana's birth that I wasn't capable or deserving of an easy birth that the fear was difficult to let go of. My friend expressed her confidence in me, suggesting that I could regain control of the pain once the "pushing phase" started. Then, after she reminded me a few times that it would take the edge off the contractions, I gratefully crawled into the warm bath she prepared. As I sat upright in the tub, my friend vigorously swished water over my belly. Labor immediately became bearable again and I was able to re-focus on my goal—a gentle and painless birth.

A few contractions later, I told my friend out of the blue that I wanted a break in the intensity of labor, and miraculously, it came. My prayers were answered with a long, contraction-free moment in which I was able to regroup and rest. Soon my body spoke again, undeniably telling me that it was time to push the baby out. It was amazing to feel my body powerfully bearing down without any conscious volition on my part. I heard my friend wonder aloud how far along I was, so I checked inside and was able to feel the head. What a delight and relief! A few seconds later, there was a gush as my water broke.

While pushing with the irresistible urge, I instinctively turned onto my hands and knees in the tub. I still remember very clearly the intense pleasure of feeling my baby's body move downward inside me. The spreading apart of my muscles and bones and the joy of voluntarily allowing my body to do its work was both arousing and exhilarating. An instant later, my friend could see the baby's head crowning, so she called John and Christiana to come into the bathroom. I was amazed to find that pinching my clitoris effectively relieved the burning sensation while I savored the soft, wet, slightly furry head of the emerging new person pressing on my eager fingers.

John came and cupped the baby's head in his hands, so I relaxed knowing she would not fall head-first into the tub. With one more contraction and three of those involuntary pushes, Angelica Marie Morgan was born into her father's hands. She was a bit purple, having birthed through the cord that had been around her neck, but soon after I turned over, rested her on my tummy, rubbed and talked softly to her, she developed a healthy color. We all felt euphoric!

John suddenly remembered the video camera then and began taping once he had wrapped the two of us in a towel and placed the hat from Christiana's birth on baby's head. When we identified and announced that the baby was a girl, Christiana, who had been standing by quietly, now exclaimed, "Baby sister! Baby sister!" I was utterly triumphant! "Pop a cork," I can be heard saying on the tape, "I feel like having a party!" as Christiana reached into the tub to gently touch her sister for the first time. Then my friend went to stir the chicken soup, leaving us to have family time alone.

I had begun making plans to get the two of us out of the still warm tub when Angelica began to root around for her first meal, so I settled back in to nurse my four-minute-old daughter. When she was done, John and my friend helped us out of the tub and dried us off. Still connected to my daughter by her umbilical cord, I energetically walked over and settled us into our family bed. Once there, Angelica and Christiana nursed together sweetly.

A few minutes later, I felt another irresistible urge to push, and out came Angelica's placenta into the disposable under-pad I had been sitting on. My friend wrapped it and gently set it alongside us. Later, I cut the cord when the babies were both contented, having finished nursing. John started making phone calls soon after, while I snuggled with my two little girls. By that time the delicious smell of chicken soup had spread throughout the house, so we all happily devoured our dinners while recalling and celebrating the afternoon's fantastic events.

My friend's recipe for chicken soup still brings back the emotions every time I make it.

Christiana and I ended the birthing day by sharing an herbal bath while Angelica acquainted herself with her father in the living room. I laughed with my friend over the irony that she had so carefully prepared the herbs to aid in healing my perineum, and I hadn't even torn. I used toilet paper without pain thirty minutes after giving birth to my delight as well. We chose not to disturb Angelica until she was well settled, so it was not until that night that we found out with my friend's brand new sling scale that she weighed 8 lbs. 14 oz. We also measured her head circumference out of curiosity, and found that it was 14 inches. A few days later we measured her at 23 inches in length. Besides enjoying my labor and birth, I was positively high long afterwards. I was delighted to find that I was remarkably energetic the entire night. I even filmed my husband interacting with his new daughter just hours later from the living room couch.

## Looking back

At first, after Angelica's birth, I wanted to tell the story and my feelings surrounding it to as many people as would listen. I assumed that women would instinctively understand what an exciting and important breakthrough my experience was, and would want to find out how to accomplish similar results themselves. What I encountered instead is that some women were threatened or angered by my story. I was called irresponsible and rude by women who claimed to be very happy with highly medicalized births. I've since come to realize that there is much more to my story than merely the mechanics. I hope that this expanded version of my story is more encouraging and informative of the alternative options in childbirth that are available and why I view them as desirable.

I am sure that one of the reasons it is so difficult for some people to hear the commentary I include in the story of Angelica's birth is that it challenges some very deeply held beliefs. Most women have had to deny their own feelings about birth and babies for years, because there are so many "experts" and well meaning, but poorly informed, friends and relatives spouting advice directly in conflict with the prompting of the heart. As a result, it is incredibly difficult to realize that your instincts and intuition about birth might have been right all along, let alone to turn around after so long. Such an awareness brings into question a whole host of other parenting practices that mothers have adopted at the insistence of "professionals." It can be very disturbing to accept that your actions may have unnecessarily hurt your child.

Simply acknowledging that you have been misled and mistreated by people you trusted is very painful. It is much easier to defend the actions of doctors and midwives, especially since that is the more acceptable thing to do by conventional standards. To embrace ideas that are as far from the mainstream as mine requires questioning a multitude of other, often deeply seated, beliefs. There is the risk for example, that you may find that your family doctor is not the most qualified to keep your family healthy. You might then face extreme pressure and hostility from your parents, in-laws, friends and family. Recognition of the truths in my critique also requires accepting a new level of responsibility that can be frightening. It is like eating the forbidden fruit in the Garden of Eden. When we know the truth, we are suddenly held accountable by our own consciences.

# 7

# *Ignorance and misinformation about birth are the norm in Western culture*

In the "modern" Western world, there is a society-wide assumption that birth is a medical event, rather than a natural occurrence. In a section of the Griesemer family's webpage (5) entitled "Interview with the author" (6), Lynn Griesemer writes, "Childbirth practices and propaganda favor the medical method of birthing, yet thousands of people across the country know that couples-birthing is safe, simple and satisfying, almost every time. Alternative birthers master their pain, fear and anxiety, while mainstream medical birthers mask the authenticity of birth through the use of drugs and technology." It's quite an unsatisfactory picture of mainstream birth Lynn paints, and sadly she's right.

In the world outside the realm of birth, people don't usually employ a medical professional unless they think that such a professional can do something for them. If a worried parent goes to all the trouble to take a sick child to the pediatrician, for example, the parent is understandably going to be disappointed if all the doctor says is, "I can't do anything for Johnny, just make sure he gets lots of rest and fluids." So, quite often what happens instead is that the good doctor prescribes an unnecessary (and possibly quite harmful in the long run) antibiotic, to make either himself or the parent feel like he's done something. And so it goes with birth. If you hire birth professionals they are quite likely to feel compelled to "treat" your condition in order to meet either your expectations or their own.

I contend that the majority of potentially birthing women don't ever consider the dangers of choosing to birth with an assistant, at least not so literally. In other words, I have heard women verbalize bad feelings about say, a particular midwife, without realizing that the midwife may have actually endangered them. Perhaps contributing to the difficulty involved in changing the modern birth standard is the common expectation that birthing "unassisted" simply means "doing nothing" in the way that many people think "not spanking" means "doing nothing" in terms of child guidance. But just as there truly are alternatives to punitive discipline, there are also alternatives to having people interfere with, and endanger, your birth.

In this society, women are also expected to be uninformed about the birth process and are often actively discouraged from gaining information that might put them at odds with the cult of medicalized birth. The assumption is that unassisted birth is dangerous or at the very least, outrageously difficult. This perspective condemns women who internalize these beliefs to have dangerous, complicated births, especially if and when they accidentally give birth unassisted. The truth is, most women can and should be able to have pleasure, safety, and an unassisted birth, too.

## What is "unassisted childbirth"?

The exact terminology for what I am attempting to describe is troublesome. Even seasoned unassisted childbirth advocates use many different descriptors for technically the same thing. What I am advocating when I suggest that the average woman consider unassisted birth, is attaining the mental, emotional and spiritual tools to be able to birth completely alone if need be, and doing so safely and confidently. In the end though, the woman should feel free to actually birth wherever and with whomever she feels most comfortable and safe when possible. Usually this makes it unnecessary to pay a professional birth assistant. For instance, I personally think I will desire to have my husband's presence while I labor and birth, but I would not consider paying an outsider for help (except perhaps a cleaning or food delivery person). The pregnant woman's goal, in my view, should be to accept full responsibility for her own safety and that of her child, and make informed choices with that aim.

Childbirth that is not assisted by professionals goes by many names. Laura Shanley simply entitled her book on the subject, Unassisted Childbirth. Lynn Griesemer, in the description of her new book called Unassisted Homebirth, An Act Of Love, refers sometimes to "raw birth." In her book, I Can Do It, Hygea Halfmoon called "it" "sovereign birth." One of the late Marylin Moran's books is entitled Pleasurable Husband/Wife Childbirth. Author Jeannine Baker coined the term, "freebirth." To describe the practice of assisting Christian women in childbirth simply with prayer and information, Carol Balizet uses the term "Zion Birth." Charity Gregson, keeper of the "Unassisted Childbirth" web site, calls "it" "do it yourself childbirth." When Valerie Nordstrom continued Marylin Moran's tradition by publishing the newsletter New Nativity II, she still called unassisted birth "couples homebirth." In the past, I personally have called it "unhindered birth."

There are many more descriptors and many, many more describers. While the philosophies behind the action may vary widely, physically it is all the same: birthing without professional or medical assistance. The actual number of participants in a birth that is not assisted by professionals varies from the woman birthing completely alone to birthing surrounded by friends and prayer teams. The essence however, is faith in the safety and normalcy of birth where the woman herself acknowledges and accepts her ultimate responsibility.

## Like it or not, birth just is unassisted

All women have unassisted births, no matter who is there with them. Birth itself is an unassisted process. It is possible for the mother and others to interfere with that process, bypass it, or even to halt it, but the process itself is involuntary. Attendants may respond to medical emergencies that occur during the birth process and treat medical problems, but they cannot assist in the process itself. Attendants only ever intervene. Contrary to popular birth practice and terminology, when someone assists a laboring woman in an emergency, s/he is still not assisting in the actual birth process.

We are taught in basic high school biology courses that some bodily functions are involuntary and some are voluntary. Involuntary functions are those that the healthy body performs automatically, without any conscious volition. Voluntary functions are those that require an act of will on the part of the person who lives in the body, or which are alterations caused by emotional imbalance. Like the beating of the heart, like the inhalation and exhalation of breath, like the brain wave activity that creates sight and hearing, birth is an involuntary activity of the female human body.

Birth happens at its own pace, in its own time, too. A pregnant woman can never know for certain when she might be birthing solo. Individuals often fool themselves that the chances of accidentally birthing unattended are slim, and perhaps when people focus all their preparation and efforts on being attended they frequently succeed. But how far should anyone realistically go in such an effort? Camping out at a hospital or midwife's house? Read a few birth stories on the internet and find out for yourself how rarely a woman's birth goes as planned or wished (7). Women make all sorts of both major and minor plans for their safety and comfort but much of it proves impossible at the time of actual birth. The too-familiar-for-comfort scenario of giving surprise birth in a taxicab, for example, is neither fun nor funny; in fact it's outright dangerous. Instead of being terrified in such an accident wouldn't it be much better for pregnant women to plan on birthing safely without assistance so that they can be pleasantly surprised if say, their sister is able to attend, or their husband gets to catch?

## What is normal, physiological birth?

Very few people actually know what normal, or physiological birth is. A 1985 World Health Organization article entitled "Having A Baby In

Europe" actually began by explaining that no one conducting the study really knew what physiological birth was because it is so rare. I find that it helps to compare other bodily functions, like breathing and bowel movement, to childbirth in order to explain the way birth is "supposed" to be. Using non-human mammalian birth as an example is another popular way to define physiological birth. However, there is much, heated debate over the question of whether humans have "instincts" or not and rightly so. Regardless, it's definitely true that the human brain has a great deal of influence on the actual outcome of birth in a way that animals do not have to cope with. So, while mammalian animals are sometimes useful models, I won't even delve into that concept.

Anthropologists are fond of making an example of "primitive" cultures where women effortlessly squat in a field, give birth, strap the baby onto their backs and go on working. One problem with this model is that it can be taken to the extreme to suggest that all women should get back to work quickly after giving birth. The truth in this legend, however, is that birth is not inherently a traumatic, medical event. By their very nature, women's bodies were created to give birth just as surely as they breathe. We can also look with discretion at how these women prepare to give birth to see why they do it so easily. One key ingredient to the women of the legend is that for the most part they are very casual about birth. In my view this is exactly the right attitude for avoiding pain, complication and debilitation.

The other truth about these women is that they don't have years of indoctrination into Western society's myth that birth is inherently dangerous and complicated. Yes, those women still have complications and their own dangerous societal myths and traditions, but what should strike western women as ironic is that theoretically, western women's births should be far better than theirs because of our advances in science and technology but they are not (8).

No matter the difficulty in defining physiological birth, what most Westerners view as normal birth is painfully far from it. In fact, it's precisely because Western society strays so far from what is physiologically normal by choice that many complications are created. Physiologically, women no more need a hospital or midwife to help them give birth than they do to pass stool everyday. Every now and then someone has trouble pooping so they go to the doctor, but until such a time we all go about our lives with the assumption that we won't have any trouble pooping, day in and day out.

Birth can and should be the same way. If, for argument's sake, we say that 95% of women's births will naturally be "normal" and 5% will naturally have complications then 95% of births should proceed thus: woman is pregnant, woman goes into labor, woman pushes baby out, woman and baby go on with life...This is physiological birth. This is exactly how simple birth can and should be for the majority of women, but most often it is not.

# 8

# *Why do people have assisted births?*

Generally, the decision to employ a professional birth assistant is a foregone conclusion; no other possibility even enters some people's minds. If it is even considered, it is usually assumed that some assistance is better than none at all. The simplest reason to have an assistant on hand during a birth is to care for the mother and child on the rare occasion that the mother is actually rendered unconscious.

It is also generally assumed that hiring a professional attendant increases the odds of a safe, uncomplicated birth mathematically, by adding to the parent's own knowledge the assistant's special training and experience through witnessing and intervening in numerous births. In addition, some parents are simply more willing to provide monetarily for the protection of themselves and their children than they are to do the work of becoming their own birth experts.

Sometimes the family's comfort (e.g. someone to rub a back, someone to talk to) and convenience (e.g. someone to clean up the mess, someone to watch older children) are even considered factors in the decision to hire a birth assistant, but usually these are clearly secondary concerns.

Those who examine their motivation to hire an assistant find many more reasons involved. Some people choose to birth with assistance purely out of fear. Fear is easily attached to birth, not only because of the importance of the newborn in our lives and our attachment to it, but also because giving birth is a moment of transformation in the woman. The act of giving birth requires a spiritual openness, a surrender that is not normal for a woman to experience every day. These changes can be made to appear mysterious and frightening by friends, relatives, and professionals with good intentions, but the wrong ideas.

Some women desire assistance because of experience or suggestions that they need to retreat into themselves during labor for various reasons including to better tolerate pain. The theory is that professional care facilitates this retreat, despite the fact that truly focusing inside one's self is much more easily done in solitude than with an audience.

All of the above are simply the most obvious reasons why women and their partners seek out birth attendants. Most people are aware of these factors to some extent. On the other hand, most people are not aware of the many dangers that surround assisted birth. In order to help parents make more informed choices for their own births I hope to show that by addressing these dangers one can simultaneously reduce the need for assistance and create a safer atmosphere for each birthing woman over all.

## Why would anyone want to give birth without attendants?

Is childbirth that is not assisted by professionals for foolhardy mavericks or safety freaks? In reality the reasons why individuals choose unassisted birth, like anything in life, run the gamut. Some women are in touch with an intuitive desire for privacy while laboring. Others have religious convictions preventing them from seeking out birth assistance. Many people first conceive of unassisted birth while searching for less financially straining options than hospital or midwife assisted birth.

Admittedly, some people must even be attracted to unassisted birth because of its novelty. Eventually though, most, if not all, who consider unassisted birth are swayed to it by the superior safety of birthing without unnecessary interference or intervention. Any superficially motivated unassisted birth may appear at the outset to be an incredibly irresponsible act. However, I hope to show that planning for unassisted birth can be one of the safest, most responsible choices out there, in which case, it really doesn't matter much how a woman and her partner find their way to it.

## How can assisted birth be merely disappointing or uncomfortable?

Because the majority of professional birth assistants have numerous protocols that require them to override the woman's desires, when a birth professional is in attendance, concessions are bound to be made. For instance, heart rate and vaginal checks are often performed at the professional's determination of "need" or convenience regardless of the woman's comfort. Some of these concessions will invariably be made at the expense of the well being of mother and/or baby. Birth attendants have lots of patients, so they use what they call "standard procedures" to make their work run smoothly. A standard procedure is something they do to all patients, with very little if any flexibility. If you don't like it, too bad.

For instance, hospitals putting the laboring woman in a wheelchair. You've probably seen this in movies. In addition to this standard procedure, birth attendants do all sorts of other harmful things to laboring women that they believe are necessary. One of the less dangerous things they usually do to all laboring women is take their blood pressure. This is done so if the woman's blood pressure is high (which is dangerous to mom and baby), the assistants can do something about it. This sounds pretty reasonable right? Well, all by itself it would be, but in almost all western births this is just the start of a huge list of standard procedures I call "interventions" that attendants require the birthing mom to have done to either herself or her baby. Some interventions cause others as in the case of high blood pressure, which has been shown to be caused by the mere entrance into a hospital.

Every single one of the following procedures is both potentially harmful to and usually unnecessary for either mother, baby, or both:

1. Drive to birthplace (either birthing family or assistants or both)

2. Wheelchair into the birthplace

3. Early admission (before labor is well established)

4. Separation from partner or friends or family

5. Replacement of clothes with gown

6. Shaving of pubic hair

7. Enema (water and/or chemicals in colon)

8. Catheterization (tube in urethra)

9. Confinement to bed

10. Forced fasting (no food or water)

11. Intravenous feeding (IV)

12. Heplock (flexible needle inserted into vein in case IV or drugs are needed later)

13. Pitocin augmentation ("pit drip"—artificial hormones to make labor stronger)

14. Cervical gel ("gelling"—pig sperm inserted into vagina to ripen cervix artificially)

15. Nipple stimulation

16. Castor oil induction

17. Herbal induction (e.g. evening primrose oil, PN6, etc.)

18. Stripping of membranes (manually separating bag of waters from cervix to stimulate labor)

19. Artificial Rupture Of Membranes/Amniotomy (manually breaking the bag of waters)

20. External Electronic Fetal Monitor (belt around waist)

21. Internal Electronic Fetal Monitor (wires screwed into baby's scalp via the vagina)

22. Cervical checks (manually feeling inside vagina for cervical openness and thinness)

23. Announcement of dilation and station (proclaiming how far along labor is)

24. Prediction of labor speed and ease

25. Time limits (protocols, standard procedures)

26. Epidural/Caudal Analgesia/Anesthesia (numbing, dulling, or changing birth sensations)

27. Direction to push or not push

28. Direction to vocalize (yell, moan, whatever)

29. Direction to be quiet

30. Direction to breathe a certain way

31. Transfer to place prepared for delivery

32. Instruction to assume lithotomy (flat on back or slightly upright) position

33. Stirrups (feet up in metal cups with legs spread wide open)

34. Sterile sheets

35. Drape (curtain or blanket placed between mother's head and bottom)

36. Disinfectant

37. Hand-strapping (tie hands down)

38. Episiotomy (cut perineum)

39. Perineal support or massage

40. Forceps extraction (tongs to pull the baby out)

41. Vacuum extraction (suction to pull baby out)

42. Cesarean Section (major abdominal surgery to get the baby out)

43. Antibiotics

44. Mirror (so mother can see the baby's head come out)

45. Delivery of baby into attendant's hands

46. Umbilical cord cut

47. Separation from newborn

48. Resuscitation (sometimes slapping or dangling) or examination of newborn

49. Interruption/denial/sabotage of breastfeeding and therefore prolactin/oxytocin stimulation and bonding

50. More time limits (for expulsion of placenta)

51. More pitocin or herbal inducements (to help placenta be expelled and uterus to contract)

52. Uterine massage (painful pushing on belly)

53. Traction on cord (pulling)

54. Manual or mechanical extraction of placenta (reaching up inside vagina or D&C)

55. Local anesthesia

56. Stitching of perineum or cesarean wound

57. Isolation

58. Bombardment with visitors

59. Extended stay at birthplace

60. Early release from birthplace

61. Wheelchair out

62. There are more.

The following interventions are more specific to the newborn:

1. Amniocentesis

2. Maternal glucose testing (heavy dose of sugar)

3. Malnutrition (via improper maternal diet counseling)

4. Ultrasound bombardment (via Ultrasound/Sonogram, and/or Doppler)

5. Palpation (feeling belly for baby's position)

6. External version (manually attempting to move baby into a different position)

7.  EFM (wires screwed into scalp)

8.  Premature birth (induction and cesarean section)

9.  Anesthesia and other drugs via placenta

10. Cesarean Section

11. Forceps extraction

12. Vacuum extraction

13. Early disruption of oxygen supply (via premature cord cutting)

14. Dangling upside down in the air

15. Slapping (to encourage breathing after oxygen has been interrupted)

16. Bright lights

17. Loud noises

18. Separation during bonding period

19. Interruption/denial/sabotage of breastfeeding

20. Apgar score (grading)

21. Washing

22. Weighing

23. Measuring

24. Prophylactic eye treatment (squirt painful and/or vision blurring stuff into eyes during critical time for eye contact with parents)

25. Vitamin K injection

26. PKU test (heel stick)

27. Bassinet/warmer

28. Artificial nipples and/or milk

29. Temperature reading (occasionally perforating rectum)

30. NICU (neo natal intensive care unit)

31. Various specifically indicated (or randomly performed) tests from spinal taps to blood work ups

32. Various specifically indicated drugs

33. Billirubin lights (jaundice treatment)

34. Antibiotics

35. Vaccination

36. Circumcision

37. Isolation

38. Bombardment with visitors

39. Extended periods of crying with no response

40. Swaddling (body wrapped tightly in blankets)

41. There are more.

Many women would simply prefer to labor in privacy but don't yet see birthing without assistance as a viable option. Even if the woman originally welcomed assistance, mismatched personalities can still end up clashing as well. Sometimes the best type of personality for prenatal care and instruction is too abrasive in the birthing room and sometimes the opposite is true. Whatever the case, the attendant may end up interfering in an unwelcome way. He or she may also bring an influential negative belief system to the birth or make the woman uncomfortable to the point where her body closes up and doesn't function properly in many other ways.

Often times, women do not feel as comfortable to move about and relax in an unfamiliar environment such as a birth center or hospital as they would at home. No matter how beautifully the walls are papered or how comfortable the furniture, there really is no place like home. Some birthing centers recognize that fancy equipment can be frightening as well, and are beginning to disguise or hide their many tools of the trade.

Further, the inherent sexuality of birth makes birthing with attendants undesirable. Imagine how a woman feels when she is really turned on and open to being sexually "penetrated." The same feeling of total relaxation and lubrication of the vaginal walls experienced in healthy sex is the absolute most conducive environment to allowing any baby to slide gently and easily into the world. An unassisted birther, and good friend of mine once wisely said, "(My husband and I) came to see birth as an intimate and sexual expression that was deserving of privacy, like trying to have orgasm while house guests are sleeping in the next room—not impossible, but more difficult to achieve" (9).

It is a shame that society requires birthing children to be such a huge financial burden, as well. New parents should be free to enjoy the birth of a new member of their family to the fullest and without fear of financial ruin. Hospitals can charge an uninsured or underinsured woman tens of thousands of dollars for even the most routine birth. Midwifery services too are made prohibitive by the fact that the thousands of dollars in fees are usually not covered by insurance at all. What's more, a freebirth, a stack of cloth diapers, a family bed, a sling carrier, and assistance with breastfeeding is all a new child really requires for the first year or more, and that only costs a few hundred dollars.

# Why does mere discomfort matter?

We may never know how many maladies of the post-partum stage, like maternal depression and infant colic, are birth-related until normal births start happening where they belong—where the woman is really most comfortable, not because of fear or misinformation, but because of true comfort: outside of the birth management realm.

Because of the ever-present mind/body connection, ignoring a woman's wishes for privacy, modesty, or freedom from unwelcome touch, becomes a hindrance to the progression of labor. Stress and its sister term distress seem to be recognized by nearly everyone for their deleterious effects on the well being of mother and child, but for some unfathomable reason they are still applied willy-nilly in labor and delivery as if they were inevitable. Surely if stress were truly inevitable, though, it would behoove attendants to minimize the unnecessary stresses we place on women in childbirth themselves! Slowing down labor is one of the absolute most harmful things you can do. The baby's heart rate is likely to drop, the woman can become exhausted from the excessive hard work and everything goes downhill from there. Fetal distress and maternal exhaustion are high on the list of reasons given for cesarean section, pitocin induction, forceps or vacuum extractions and fundal pressure.

Planned, midwife-attended homebirths have been proven to be statistically safer (Goer, Kitzinger, Marjorie, Stewart) than hospital birth, but hard facts aside, when determining the success of one method of birth, one must also examine the definition of success. Is satisfaction an important part of the birth experience, and if so how does unassisted homebirth differ from attended birth? For example, should an inevitable death be considered a success if it was peaceful and loving? Those who have unfortunately experienced both hospital and home death can attest to the additional stress and anxiety that a medical environment produces. In such a time of unfathomable grief, surely it is best to soften the blow as much as possible.

Women's emotional enrichment is easily minimized in comparison to aspects of physical safety, but the two are steadfastly intertwined. A woman's emotional state directly influences the safety of her birth because the body responds directly to one's beliefs both positively and negatively (10). Women can literally close their vaginas against the exit of a child both unintentionally and intentionally. This power was put there to allow the woman to avoid birthing in more obviously unsafe conditions like when wild animals are attacking. But to the primal mind of the birthing woman, even a birth attendant whose desires are in conflict with hers is a legitimate threat.

Aside from the impact a woman's satisfaction has on her safety, the empowerment of unassisted birth is important in and of itself. There is something very crucial to birthing one's own children that impacts the whole woman, her partner, and all her children, not to mention the gently birthed child, for years to come. Women experienced in birthing unassisted will tell you that their marriages are strengthened (Moran) and their personal confidence, happiness, and faith is increased greatly. Gentle-born children may be more intuitive and flexible and are definitely bonded more closely with their parents (LeBoyer). These phenomena may be directly related to the opiate effect of the endorphins naturally present in the bodies of mother and baby at birth; as Michel Odent says in the article "Why Laboring Women Don't Need Support" (11), "It's well known that opiates induce a state of dependency. When mother and baby haven't yet eliminated their endorphins and are close to each other, the beginning of a deep bond is created. In fact, when sexual partners are close to each other and impregnated with opiates, another kind of bonding may result that follows exactly the same model as the bonding between mother and baby."

Gayle Peterson writes, "Because our culture devalues that which is feminine, even the most intimate and basic processes of women's lives become targets for judgment" (12). We must not let the question of empowerment be brushed aside by a few with disparaging assertions that it is a "feminist" issue and therefore unimportant to those not concerned with political correctness. It is time we all honestly asked ourselves, "Is it right that the emotional is subjugated by the physical?" This is a patriarchal standard, and not a safe one for a spiritual event like birth. Just why is a beating heart viewed by society as more important than the torture of the innocent individual (via "heroic" life saving efforts)? Most people would probably agree that this is a complicated and individual decision that is best made by the parents in each situation. The problem lies in the fact that parents today are not making truly informed decisions when the option of unassisted birth; even unassisted death is never presented as an option. It's never fair to second guess the grief of parents who did what they knew to do at the time, but it's also only fair to begin fully informing parents of their options today.

# 9

# *The dangers of assisted birth*

Most consumers of birth services do not realize how detrimental it can truly be to retain a birth attendant, and so end up dangerously, uncomfortably, or just unnecessarily manipulated and interfered with during labor. All this is done in the name of having "someone" attend in a professional capacity "just in case." Some hypothetical benefit is usually imagined. The equation of 'assistant+couple=safer birth' is not exactly flawed to the core. Too many people simply never take into account the many subtractions from the benefits of assisted birth when analyzing the risk to-benefit-ratio. Attendants can easily endanger a laboring woman. This is not to say that they do it intentionally. Many attendants and the parents themselves plainly lack a true understanding of normal, physiological birth. The many risks of birthing attended can, for the most part, be divided into the two ways the practice deviates from the physiological ideal: mentally/emotionally/spiritually and physically.

## Emotional dangers of birthing assisted

It has been said before that a woman is safest birthing where she feels safest, and this is true. It's also true, however, that most women choose their birth attendant out of fear and not of true comfort. Most people are tremendously uninformed about the safety of prepared unassisted homebirth. Women who feel safest in an environment where they are actually endangered are at risk for horrendous complications.

All births have the very real potential of ending up unassisted or at least assisted differently than planned. The belief that one cannot birth safely alone has the potential to endanger one's labor in and of itself should one end up laboring alone. The same concept also holds true in any unpredicted circumstances including a different attendant, different location, and different style of labor. The underlying reason is that the woman's body responds according to her beliefs either negatively or positively.

Hiring a birth attendant does nothing to guarantee the safety of birth, despite the reasoning most people use to explain seeking them out. The fact is that if women relax because they are assisted then they are more likely to have subtle problems go unnoticed. Because the birthing woman is her own best expert, believing one's assistant will catch any and all problems is just as dangerous as administering a whole host of invasive tests. To neglect to consult with the one greatest source of wisdom about a particular birth is obviously to flirt with disaster. Similarly, birth plans are wonderful things to have written up in case of the worst, but they too encourage reliance on something that is often ignored, forgotten, or rushed through in an emergency.

When either the birthing woman or her attendants (partners included) revere "experience" over the woman's innate inner wisdom, that experience can easily become more dangerous than beneficial. For instance, a woman's body may tell her to assume a position that her midwife's experience tells her is not safe or is merely inconvenient. This sounds outrageous, and it is, but it happens all the time. The woman's body may be preparing the best passage for birth with this particular position (squat for breech presentation, for instance), but because of the assistant's presence there is a conflict, which must be resolved. Does the woman argue with her paid help while in labor? Women do this all the time, but when a woman is defensive, her body (and therefore the baby's) can be flooded with stress hormones, increasing the heart rate and blood pressure, creating tension and therefore pain, etc. Or should the woman second guess her body and live with the consequences?

The signs of labor's stages (dilation, for instance) can change radically in a short amount of time. Therefore, when an "expert" assesses and announces their interpretation of "where" a woman is in labor, and that assessment conflicts with what her body tells her, the news can easily become a depressing self-fulfilling prophecy. The woman then becomes disheartened and exhausted completely unnecessarily.

Because of the fact that an outsider's fears are easily transferred onto the spiritually open birthing woman, the experiences that birth attendants bring with them can also be a hindrance and therefore a danger. This is especially true when the assistant's experiences are of pain and complication. A fearful attendant exhibits both subtle and clear evidence of their true emotions. As adrenaline elevates, movements quicken and stiffen, the voice becomes strained, and eyes widen. If it's difficult to hide fear from the average person, it is impossible to hide it from a laboring woman. What is worse is that the attendant is usually expected by all parties to be an emotional anchor. The attendant's fear therefore becomes the laboring woman's fear, which allows tension, pain, and complications to set in (Read).

There is an important though subtle difference between someone who is paid specifically to attend a birth because of her/his expertise and someone who is solely emotional and/or physical support. It's plainly difficult not to assist a woman when she is working hard or appears to be in pain. It is especially difficult not to use "special" training and hi-tech, expensive equipment when it is available. As I explain in my introduction, the expectations of both clients and attendants weigh heavily on the side of interventions, whether they are needed or not, based solely on the fact that a service is being paid for. The rationale is that if money has been exchanged for a service, then surely a service must be performed.

Some people suggest that the birth attendant's lack of emotional involvement is an asset, but I question this logic. Hopefully any attendant has a genuine concern for the welfare of his/her clients, but no impartial observer can replace the intuition of an informed and intentionally, actively involved parent.

Another concern is that the bonding feelings of pride, empowerment, and victory that are often shared amongst the attendants at a birth may be more appropriately kept within the family unit. For reasons explained above and more, it's not uncommon for a woman to feel gratitude towards her obstetrician or midwife to the painful exclusion of her partner. This is surely detrimental to the primary relationship, which is in turn harmful to the child.

Finally, birthing with assistance has a great deal of potential to rob a woman of confidence in her body for future births. Many women seeking safer births find the need to "deprogram" themselves from their past assistants' fears and beliefs. For instance, it's not uncommon for a woman who has had a cesarean for CPD to be nagged with the fear that her body really is too small to birth a baby. Make no mistakes, there is no more confident a birthing woman than one who has already experienced a planned birth that was not assisted by professionals.

## Some dangers aren't quite so clearly either physical or emotional and some are both.

Due to concerns for litigation and convenience of routine, among other reasons, almost all professional birth attendants have and use what are called protocols, or standard procedures. A standard procedure is one that has been established for use on all patients in specified scenarios, with very little flexibility. A protocol is similarly a predetermined plan for treatment. For instance, many attendants have a rule describing the acceptable length of pregnancy before emergency plans are set in motion. For most attendants this means inducement of labor in some form and for midwives this usually includes a point where the woman is eventually referred to a hospital for more aggressive treatment.

Standard procedures and protocols endanger the women who are affected by specific protocols, those whose pregnancies progress beyond the stated limit, for example, because of the stress this emergency status places on them, the change of caregiver that often results, and the risks involved in greater intervention. Even the women who are not directly impacted by protocols are regularly distressed by the fear of the consequences of going over the limits. But why should a woman who is already in danger be subjected to more stress and more intervention? If she is really in danger should she not be pampered and comforted and her risks reduced? The fact is, "high risk" patients are at even higher risk for being endangered by interventive attendants, via over-monitoring, transmissive paranoia, dangerous testing and over-application of intervention, and are especially safer birthing unhindered.

Another danger of assisted birth is that specific attendants are frequently unavailable at the exact moment of birth. All too often, women end up birthing with the "backup" caregiver or worse, a complete stranger. Even when one's choice of assistant is fulfilled at the moment of birth, it's simply impossible to predict every outcome and brief a birth attendant on all your desires for each situation in advance. It is also impossible to ensure that the birth assistant is similarly informed and in agreement with a couple's beliefs, 100%, in all areas of birth. Every single person has a different opinion on what is and is not safe. Let's face it, even married couples don't agree on most birth practices 100%. For instance, some people think potent drugs are safe; others think that injecting blood products like Rhogam without proof that it will improve the outcome is desirable. Because of the unpredictability of birth, if you choose to birth with an attendant, to get your wishes respected you would either have to be unusually coherent and strong (which is understandably difficult and uncomfortable, and, hence, dangerous), unusually lucky, or you would have to bend somewhere.

# Physical dangers of birthing assisted

Unlike members of one's immediate family, birth attendants, whether in their own territory or in the home of the birthing couple, invariably carry bacteria which is potentially dangerous due to being foreign to mother and child. Whereas the mother's body is accustomed to family germs and providing important immunities for her and her baby, outsiders' germs are always a potential threat to both. This is especially of concern when the assistant requires the mother to submit to vaginal exams at any time.

The birthing assistant's very presence is physically dangerous to the birthing woman as well. Michel Odent explains that all the hormones released during labor originate from the neocortex (11). Because of the inhibiting effect on labor it is important not to stimulate this part of the woman's brain while she is giving birth. The neocortex is easily stimulated by anything that causes an adrenaline rush, or merely by talking to the woman, turning on bright lights, watching or observing her, and the like.

Finally, birth assistants are geared toward emergencies either by training, or mere expectation, and in preparation for those emergencies they often create their own. This is the phenomenon I refer to when I use the phrase "dangerous interventions." This is also referred to as an iatrogenic emergency or snowball effect. Here are some examples of how common interventions can be dangerous.

1.  Many women on homebirth email lists report experiencing premature rupture of membranes directly following routine vaginal checks. Standard procedures for premature rupture of membranes often include emergency protocols like artificial induction of labor within a predetermined number of hours. This can lead to cesarean section due to lack of progress (when the body is not ready to give birth sometimes it just won't give birth!), or premature birth, among other things.

2. Untold numbers of women have weaned their babies unnecessarily due to a common birth intervention. It is not well known, but routine administration of antibiotics (for cesarean section or high temperature, for instance, sometimes without the parents' knowledge) has a detrimental effect on breastfeeding. Antibiotics disturb the delicate balance of healthy yeast in the body, creating an over growth. This over growth of yeast is commonly known as thrush. A thrush infection of the breasts can cause extremely severe nipple pain. With thrush infection, regular methods of relieving nipple pain will not work. If no diagnosis is made or treatments given then breastfeeding may be abandoned altogether as being too painful.

3. Amniocentesis, D&C, pulling on the umbilical cord, pushing on the uterus (fundal pressure) and manual extraction of the placenta can cause hemorrhage and/or Rh sensitization (Mendelsohn).

4. The typical drugs used in a professionally assisted birth have a plethora of dangerous effects (13). The Physician's Desk Reference (14) says that epidurals (whose drug composition actually varies from one hospital to the next, often times including narcotics without the parents' awareness) do in fact reach the baby, and their safety has not been proven. Most drugs commonly used during labor have pages of contraindications. Examples are the artificial form of oxytocin—pitocin, and progesterone cervical gel, among whose many contraindications are 1. Elective induction, 2. Obstetrical emergencies where the benefit-to-risk ratio for either the fetus or the mother favors surgical intervention, 3. Fetal distress, 4. Failure to progress, 5. Hypersensitivity to the drug, 6. History of cesarean section, 7. History of difficult labor and/or traumatic delivery, 8. Ruptured membranes, and more. It's interesting to note that the effects of both these and many pain relieving drugs can be duplicated in the privacy of one's own home. Nipple stimulation and other natural components of foreplay and lovemaking, while pro-

viding pain-relieving relaxation, also produce oxytocin in perfectly safe amounts. Vaginally applied (via coitus) and orally ingested semen also provide a safe and more palatable form of progesterone than the pig sperm inserts that hospitals currently use.

5. The positions birth attendants require or simply ask women to labor/birth in can be detrimental to the goal of a healthy mom/baby outcome. Laboring on your back or reclining literally closes the pelvic opening most dangerously, second only to hanging upside down. Such positioning also reverses the benefits of gravity completely, so that the woman's body is not only pushing her baby without the help of gravity, but upward against it.

6. Vaginal exams both introduce dangerous foreign bacteria into the birth canal, and also slow down labor for two reasons. The first is psychological. Obviously it is unnatural to have strangers put their hands inside of you, let alone in public, and let alone when you are doing one of the most special, most personal things in the world: birthing a baby. The second is physical. The only way a baby can come out is if the vagina and cervix are 100% open. Most women have extreme difficulty relaxing before, during, and after vaginal exams.

7. Cesarean section is major surgery, and, as with other surgical procedures, involves a lot of risks. The more serious of these are laceration, infection, excessive blood loss, reactions to anesthesia, premature birth, lack of compression in birth canal and other fetal injury.

8. Even seemingly minor interventions can have great repercussions. Take the IV for example. First they have to interrupt the precious concentration of the laboring woman to insert a needle. Then, if neither option of an uncomfortable hep-lock or wheeling an IV pole around like a sick person is available, the woman will have to stay in bed while she labors. Either way, the attendants are most

likely going to ask the woman to lie down every half-hour or so to hook her up to a monitor for a while. However, since walking is one of the best ways to help labor progress well, being stuck in bed for any reason can artificially slow down labor, which in turn can cause fetal distress, which in turn can lead to one of the more radical interventions. It's like an avalanche that begins with a pebble. Hence the term, "snowball effect."

9.  Other interventions are more indirectly responsible for either slowing down labor's progress, or making it too fast for the mom to handle. Amniotomy, for instance, introduces foreign bacteria into the vagina (which everyone knows is bad to do with ruptured membranes) and unnaturally speeds up labor, sometimes causing fetal distress, which leads to induction, which leads to premature birth, which necessitates neonatal intensive care….And on the ball rolls.

## What about Midwifery?

Midwives have long been the patron saints of the homebirth community. The feeling among homebirthers is generally that professional midwifery is invaluable in empowering women and providing them with safe births, and so must be protected. What isn't well represented is the fact that midwifery cannot simultaneously provide women with true faith in birth and continue to be necessary. Why can't a midwife's presence be that of a caring friend and not of a commanding professional? The problem lies in the fact that midwifery is a business based on referrals and repeat clients alone. If each midwife truly empowered her clients then the majority wouldn't need her.

The small amount of unassisted birthers in the world may not threaten midwifery in general but the unassisted birth movement is certainly a threat to individual midwives! So, individual midwives must guard themselves against personal career obsolescence. This is especially critical to a woman who has poured her own money and years of blood, sweat, and tears into her training and practice while facing heavy criticism from mainstream society all the way.

Some people will insist that there is a difference between midwives that interfere in the ways that I describe above and the practice of Direct Entry (or Lay) Midwifery. It is important to note that the midwives I have had very negative experiences with (15) were DEM's. I had done my research when I paid them to attend me. They said all the right things when I interviewed them. They claimed and still claim to believe in everything I believed in regarding the dangers of intervention. They had attended over 2,000 births. They were widely published. Their articles and books expressed agreement with my beliefs, too. They are highly respected in the midwifery community even today. (I recently read Nancy Cohen referring to one of these women as a dear friend...) I have seen their books and articles recommended on many Internet homebirth bulletin boards & email lists. These facts, in addition to the volumes of birth stories on the internet describing various DE/lay midwifery interventions, are what has brought me to warn women about midwives despite their reputation. On the other hand, I do not in any way intend to generalize that all midwives are interventive.

## What do you have against midwives anyway?

As a staunch and vocal advocate of the unassisted birth movement, this is a question that I am asked quite often in one form or another. I'm sure that even some of my sister unassisted birthers must wonder at times whether my firm non-support of midwifery isn't a bit overboard. I want to address this concern because there are some very good reasons behind my position that should be considered by anyone with a birth in their future, in order that they may make the most informed discussions about whether or not to invite attendants.

Not long ago, I was very interested to read an article posted on a somewhat progressive online parenting bulletin board. This article was written by a midwife and was, according to its title, supposed to be about unassisted birth but was essentially this woman explaining her belief in what she called, (I'm paraphrasing) "a spiritual basis for the wholeness of a woman-centered experience." This particular post was, unfortunately, permanently deleted after I read it. But the essence of this woman's point in short, was that she supported unassisted birth for those who want it, but that she believed that—for her at least and perhaps for many other women—childbirth is naturally a time when women need other women to provide invaluable support and love for one another.

I hope that it is clear by now that, in many ways, I too sincerely value the ages old tradition of women caring for and supporting one another in birth. So, it won't be surprising that I agreed with much of that midwife's original article. However, I wasn't at all surprised or comforted to read yet another midwife extolling the virtues of the traditional concept of birth as a "woman-centered" experience. Like many others before her, and many to come, this midwife regurgitated the stereotype that childbirth is just a "women's thing." I grew up in a feminist household (my lesbian mother taught Women's Studies at Arizona State University for fifteen years, took me to gay rights marches, had me speak to her classes about growing up straight with a lesbian mother, etc.) so I think I'm pretty open-minded and well versed in such things. But even considering this unusual background, it still seems only logical to me that birth should actually be a family centered experience. One in which women who are not the birthing woman's life partner are extraneous.

In other words, it seems to me that any male babies and male partners involved are at least equally important as, if not more important than any "outside" female, no matter how emotionally close the two women may be. I admit that this view is rather traditional, and not very inclusive of such lifestyles as polygamy and such, but I'm not trying to be discriminatory here. Rather, I'm just not really trying to "go there" in this particular train of thought.

Don't get me wrong though, please. It's not that I don't think non-family women have a crucial role to play in childbirth! It's just that, as I said once before, "many women aren't actually benefited by having a third party present in their house to fulfill [the] ancient role [of "wise woman birth support"] for them, but the information and support should still be readily available and acceptable for them." Along these lines I was really intrigued by a response to the above mentioned midwife's post. In it, the author described a "ring of female protection within about twenty feet..." as her vision of the ideal birth support.

While the author of this quote may have meant it literally, this "ring" seems perfectly symbolic of the type of relationship I have acquired and nurtured with my unassisted childbirth advocate friends. We, a family of nearly 270 women at the last count, protect, support, and help one another very powerfully, and yet invisibly—through loving correspondence—rather than hands-on in one another's birth space. The same respondent to the midwife's article also depicted the ideal support as a "birthing co-op," the wording of which set all kinds of bells ringing in me, because I had been working very hard lately to nurture something very much like that. As you read further, you will see how my dream and efforts gradually came to fruition.

While that subject deserves an entire chapter dedicated to itself alone, I just wanted to point out concretely that unassisted birth is absolutely not about giving birth without support or resources. To return to the subject of midwifery and woman centered birth, the aforementioned midwife spoke, as many do, of her support for women during childbirth through midwifery as being about "love," as though unassisted birth was somehow lacking in that aspect. But for myself and many other women, not having any birth attendant, be that a "holistic" midwife or otherwise, is about love too.

Unassisted birth is just focused on the love in what I would describe as the "primary" or parental relationship and the family as a whole, rather than that between two women (unless we're talking about lesbian couples). A woman and her partner (if she has one) conceive a child (even if through "artificial" means) out of their love for one another and their potential offspring. Personally, I am not ashamed to say that I value those two familial bonds above any others. Call me prudish or conservative if you will (Ha!), but there it is. To me it just seems both practically and spiritually natural that the act of receiving a child is just as private, sexual, intimate, what have you, as conceiving that child once was.

As I openly and honestly share the horror story of my personal experiences with midwives, many people may be inclined to think that I have merely lost my objectivity. So, before anyone gets the impression that I think all midwives are manipulative, interventive creeps, let me clarify. I understand that it's tempting to dismiss my new-found passion for unassisted childbirth as simply going overboard the other way. This is truly an unfortunate thing! In fact, I really, truly believe that all the midwives I've ever met, including those who I would describe as having raped me, are and were well meaning! My perspective is just that, along with having negative experiences that have proven valuable to share, I happen to have acquired an unusually keen perception of how truly interventive (whether intentional or not) midwifery itself really is. I can honestly say that I have considered it seriously and in depth over a long period of time, and I do have some evidence to support my belief that I am not, in fact, unusually biased against midwives, or holding a distorted view of them.

First, I'd like to re-emphasize that it wasn't until long after my dramatically negative experiences that I started identifying them as such. It was somewhere in the middle of my second pregnancy that I started to connect negative emotions to my first birth. That would be nearly two years later. If nothing else, the fact that I hired and paid one of those very same midwives with the intention of having her attend my second birth should show that I held on to my denial pretty strongly for a while.

Secondly, it wasn't just me that was blinded in the beginning. From my mother's account of Christiana's birth—which I personally approved and mailed out just three days after—you can see that I definitely wasn't the only one that rationalized the very negative behavior of the midwives. There were 3 midwives, my friend—a childbirth educator in training as a midwife, my husband, and my mother there who all agreed with my original assertion that that was a beautiful, empowering birth.

This isn't all my evidence, however. There were two other important factors that led me to my current belief that the problems I experienced and the denial I went through weren't just limited to the few midwives I had come in contact with. What happened was that I literally gained a whole new perspective on childbirth altogether. First, by reading Laura Shanley's book Unassisted Childbirth, and second by actually birthing my second daughter Angelica unhindered.

If you look at the list of childbirth interventions I include in chapter eight, you will see that I included many items that are not generally considered interventions. What I have come to understand is that these are all in fact potentially inhibiting (and therefore dangerous) to birth. Perineal support and massage, which are considered by most to be a very non-interventionist way to prevent perineal tears, are good examples. Actually, any touching in this very private area by non-lovers can be uncomfortable and therefore inhibitive, which ultimately constitutes a danger to the laboring woman and her baby. Admittedly, every such intervention is only problematic in varying degrees (sometimes minuscule) and others only so in specific circumstances, but what I have come to understand is that we must always keep in mind the equation: how much is too much intervention in addition to everything else?

Anyway, I was still under the impression that many people who read my story today are—that my experiences with the violating midwives were unusual—when with my new perspective, I started watching birth videos, and reading and listening to birth stories by the hundreds. It was not until then that I accidentally noticed, one by one, a common thread that I had never noticed before. What I started to notice is that homebirth stories are literally riddled with the above mentioned interventions. Not only that, but I started to find that the same interventions were either being downplayed and/or glorified in almost every single homebirth story I read, even the same ones I had read a few years before and found uplifting and empowering. Honestly, it was a shocking revelation to me, not an expected support of some preconceived notion that midwives are all evil, as some people might have guessed.

I'd also like to say that while I do think that midwives are quite often interventive, if I haven't made it clear enough already, I sincerely believe that this is mostly due to an inevitability involved in attended birth itself that can't be helped and almost never anything malicious or intended by individual midwives. Most people who have had unassisted births (and I personally know an unusually large number of them) understand the many benefits of unassisted birth and the risks of attended birth and are strong advocates for UC. Rather than depending and trusting in "training", "techniques" and the like, most unassisted birthers trust that birth proceeds well on its own. Most hold a high degree of trust and respect for women's ability to make good choices about their own births too, and therein lies the basis for their acceptance of full personal responsibility.

But midwifery training itself almost can't help but instill subtle fear and distrust in other women's bodies into a person because essentially it is preparation for complications. This is not a judgment! I know many midwives who very valiantly guard against internalizing such fears, but the good ones all admit that it is a great challenge. Also, if you have complete trust in birth then you understand that reliance on "assistants" inhibits the process. It's impossible to simultaneously feel necessary and unnecessary, so for a midwife to continue being a midwife rather than encouraging unassisted birth, a compromise must be made. In my experience this usually occurs as a (usually very subtle) lack of faith in one's clients. I've heard perfectly well-meaning midwives rationalize over and over that "some women just aren't (fill in the blank: ready, willing, able, etc.) to give birth unassisted." If you follow this belief—this attempt to be the judge of another person's heart—to its natural conclusion, then you can't help women become ready, willing, or able either.

For an example of why even the holistic, loving tradition of midwifery (not "med" wifery) is interventive to its very core, consider the fact that men can't give birth. Therefore, any view that women need experience and understanding support in labor just automatically devalues the father's role. This usually plays out as fathers being relegated to the sidelines of mere physical support in birth. I personally view this as a very negative intervention. The late Marylin Moran wrote a book called Pleasurable Husband/Wife Childbirth, in which she makes an incredibly powerful argument that any birth attendant (loving, holistic, or not—not just medically interventive ones) endangers—not only the birth process itself—but also the family and partner love bonds. There is some other really off the wall stuff in her book that I don't necessarily agree with, but on this one point I do.

It would require writing a whole new book to explain all the supporting evidence for this theory of Marylin's, but I think I can give a descriptive example. Just as Michel Odent has documented that the neocortex of the laboring woman is negatively stimulated (inhibiting labor) by any outside interaction—from touch to eye contact—he has also documented a more readily accepted phenomenon of a literal chemical bonding of the attendants of birth to one another. To paraphrase Odent's explanation, the hormones that flow through a woman's body during labor and birth have an opiate effect on her. Just as opiates are addictive, these hormones are also addictive, so that whomever is closest to the woman as she labors and births is very literally bonded with her.

Lest anyone get the impression that I think so highly of Michel Odent that I can't be objective about his work, I just want to say that while I think it's cool that someone "respected" has studied and drawn conclusions about this stuff, really his work just makes a lot of sense to me. Anyway, in my personal opinion, the only people that should rightly be at the receiving end of such intense, life long attachment power are the woman's partner and her baby. If you read enough birth stories you find out that instead, there is a very common occurrence of women having crushes on their OB's and similarly strong attachments to their midwives, to such an extent that they experience confusion at the intensity of these feelings and sometimes even depression once the professional relationship necessarily ends.

Finally, I want to emphasize that I do not intend all this to promote the epidemic of male partners being birth "coaches" ala, "Come on honey, BREATHE!!! Yeah, that's the way, ONE, TWO, THREE. Keep your chin down. You can do it! FOUR, FIVE, SIX…" Nor am I advocating for husbands to become midwives: nurturing, intuitive birth "experts." This may come naturally for the rare man, but not only is this just as potentially harmful to birth as female midwifery, I also don't think that the fact that the average man will never fit this nurturing intuitive mold should minimize his role in his partner's birth. What I do recommend is for the male partner to be a true partner in labor. In individual people's lives this may mean being the mother's lover and/or protector of both his partner and babies, but most importantly it should be what comes naturally. Assisted birth is simply not conducive to men readily accepting and enjoying these roles.

## What about being assisted by friends?

Hopefully I've already demonstrated that friends can be equally as dangerous as any other birth assistant can, for many reasons. Most obvious is the fact that lay people are usually less informed than even the average birthing couple and they may panic or simply interfere unintentionally. Ironically, some friends may not interfere with birth until long after the fact, when occasionally they may feel inclined to take credit for "saving" the laboring woman, or giving her more assistance than she actually needed. Birth is an incredibly private and personal event, so no one in their right mind would share such a moment with someone who they had any inkling would turn against them. The sad truth, however, is that relationships change and friends grow apart even more often than marriages. If anyone ever wanted to hurt another, the intimate details of a birth story, photos, and video entrusted to friends are easily shared inappropriately or stolen. I mention this only so that prospective parents who are assessing their options can beware.

## Is assisted birth inherently, inevitably, or unavoidably dangerous?

If we can agree again for argument's sake that 95% of births could be normal and uncomplicated without outside interference, and then to the normal births add 5% of women who could be assisted by technology, we should come up with, essentially, no complicated births. Our modern scientific advances should easily be helping that small segment of women rather than creating more complications. If there is no improvement, then there is just a tradeoff of one complication for another and since leaving the inevitable tragedies at home in loving comfort might actually be better by most people's standards than having them happen in an interventive environment, the tradeoff is actually worse. With everything as it is today, technology isn't even making births a little bit better. There is just no over all advantage. Yes, some individual births that would naturally be complicated may be better attended by a midwife or obstetrician than unattended with the same amount of faith and information, but not over all and not better than having 95% of births be prepared, trusting, unassisted birth.

# 10

## *How can unassisted childbirth be safe?*

Women who have only ever experienced or heard examples of assisted birth or accidental unassisted birth will understandably have little if any confidence that their bodies are actually capable of giving birth unassisted. If you are one of these women it is important to keep in mind that the many anecdotal examples of complication are only attributable to the fact that very few people ever even try prepared, informed, unassisted birth.

Stories of people who somehow ended up birthing unintentionally unassisted and consequently suffered horrible complications are often brought up in an attempt to prove that unassisted birth is unsafe, but they are clearly poor excuses for an argument. Choosing not to prepare ones self to birth one's own baby is exactly what causes the problems such people encountered. Many people talk a good game about being prepared in case of an emergency and yet, when the possibility of birthing unassisted is figured in, they were not indeed fully prepared. So these people simply illustrate my point. There is no harm done by addressing anecdotal situations, in fact determining causes of complication can be quite helpful for illustrating how a situation could be handled differently for the sake of future babies. On the other hand these examples are not valid as disproof.

Presumably average parents are competent enough to care for their offspring without professional supervision from at least a few days after birth until age eighteen, right? So what is it about birth that makes everyone so terrified that something horribly unpredictable will happen in those first few hours and days? Yes, babies and mothers sometimes die in the process of birth, but people die in car accidents much more frequently and parents still drive home from hospitals and birthing centers without batting an eyelash! The tremendous fear that surrounds birth is absolutely senseless.

The woman's body was literally made to give birth without assistance, so it's not necessary (I'm not suggesting that it's not sometimes desirable, just not necessary) to hire an assistant to make up for a woman's lack of experience. Without any voluntary effort on the part of the mother, the uterus will push the baby out, all by itself. Michel Odent (11) describes what he calls the, "fetus ejection reflex." This ejection reflex, Odent explains, is a physiological process facilitated by an important release of hormones in the last stage of labor that only occurs "when the birth is unguided and undisturbed." It is also well known that nature's wisdom provides for the baby, who will "crawl" to the breast on its own if left unhindered.

Midwife, childbirth educator, and author Nancy Wainer Cohen wisely says, "Birth is not a medical circumstance. We get in trouble because we just don't understand this concept. We are mammals. Mammals birth their babies! Women are strong capable human beings who are fully able to deliver their babies" (16). Our bodies know how to do countless normal, natural, life essential functions (breathing, pumping blood, eating, sleeping, peeing, pooping, forming baby in womb, nourishing a baby, etc. as opposed to medical procedures like orchestrated birth) without any outside assistance. We all occasionally have difficulties with various essential functions of our bodies and at those times we go to specialists for those disorders and we either do just fine the rest of the time or there is an occasional unavoidable death (which is always tragic). Birth need not be any different. The average birth is not a disorder, but most are treated as such. Again, I encourage the reader to peruse a few birth stories on the Internet and try to find more than a handful where there wasn't some "emergency" that the attendant corrected. Are that many women's bodies so seriously flawed? I think not.

## Why are women qualified to give birth?

Hopefully I have shown that in order to be safe, birthing women have to be comfortable, aware, informed, in tune, and on guard no matter whom they invite to assist them, if anyone. Taking full responsibility for your own safety places you in the unique position of being more in tune and aware of the needs of your own body, your unborn child's and your newborn's than you would otherwise be if you relied in advance on assistance. As an example, think of the passengers on an airplane. If you could know in advance that you would be flying a plane without a pilot, you would surely prepare a lot more than if you just planned on being a passenger. Childbirth is the same way. Getting pregnant in the first place should alert a woman to the fact that she might have to birth alone.

The idea that anyone other than the woman in labor can be more expert at birthing her very own baby is preposterous. No "expert" who has spent the majority of her/his time studying problems is going to know more about a woman than she herself when she has focused attention and energy on her fears, her body, etc. No amount of training, witnessing, or book learning can help a body birth a baby (sometimes deprogramming from the "wrong" education is even required), but that's because the body was physically made to do its job, not because experience is required to birth. Only you will know when and where you need to eat, drink, toilet, sleep, push, not push, squat, walk, dance, make love, stand up, lie down, etc. If you give the job of running your birth to anyone else, you will end up with that person's version of what your birth should be. Make no mistake; this is the danger women need to be aware of.

To agree that an outsider's "experience" is something better than what all women have available inside them would be to deny the normal state of the female body and continue a vicious cycle of misinformation and distrust in the birth process. Witnessing, studying for, and participating in countless births cannot make an attendant choose to do the right thing. Yes, our own beliefs about birth can get in the way and endanger our births just as easily as an assistant's, but that is why it's important to inform women and reach out rather than lying down and accepting birth management.

There's no substitute for a mother's "intuition" (if you will) either, especially for catching problems that are not obvious to the naked eye. Subtle problematic symptoms may even be best caught by informed parents who are concerned and in tune, but not fearful. Intuition is strong and ingrained in us but it must not be dulled by reliance on out-siders. The international breastfeeding support and information orga-nization, La Leche League, advocates that parents themselves care for newborns right from the start rather than allowing them to be whisked away to the nursery. This is because this experience increases confi-dence and familiarity. The parents who make an unfettered effort to understand their own newborn from the very moment of birth become more acutely aware of more subtle nuances of behavior that may indi-cate a problem. Also, again, accepting responsibility for one's own wel-fare encourages parents to act more responsibly.

Caring parents with the right information can notice any condition that is noticeable and they certainly shouldn't be blamed for missing any others. Almost all of what unassisted birthers would do in a "real" emergency is exactly the same as what they would do if they had a mid-wife attending at home (for example call 911, go to a hospital, use herbs, etc.), but some of it is definitely better. One has to decide how far one wants to go in the name of looking for problems "just in case." Should we do X-ray's, CAT scans and spinal taps on every newborn? Should we put our births in danger by employing a birth assistant just in case they might find a problem we would miss? Remember the equa-tion I described before and ask yourself, where does it stop?

# When is unassisted childbirth unsafe?

As I have shown, attendants can easily endanger a laboring woman. This is not to say that not having an attendant might not also endanger the same woman. Again, a woman's own beliefs alone can make birthing unassisted dangerous. The truth is, so long as a woman believes that she needs professional assistance to birth, then she does. The idea that women inherently require assistance during labor is only a dangerous myth reinforced by television, movies and common gossip, but when women believe the myth, they play the part. Hopefully I've made it obvious that such a belief system is fertile ground for complications and must be challenged and resolved before unassisted birth can be safely attempted.

In addition, merely having the knowledge and ability to birth safely unassisted inside you isn't the same as being aware of it and/or using it. I personally had to purposefully deprogram myself of years of harmful beliefs that women's bodies need assistance in labor, and hours of similarly disempowering messages from the midwives I hired to attend my first birth. Just knowing with my head that my body could birth didn't make me believe it, and believing it didn't make me use the knowledge and power within me during labor. All of us always have the choice to use our heads over our hearts. That's called free will.

There is also a very large difference between overconfidence in ability and humble faith in the power that designed the female body. Just as confidence can be misplaced in the wrong attendant, confidence can also be misplaced in training and knowledge. With faith, on the other hand, one is reassured that even though laboring women and their babies are sometimes hurt, even when we've done our best to prevent it, there is surely a reason and a plan for it to be used for some ultimate good.

Sadly, some people make the incorrect assumption that birthing without medical assistance is equivalent to doing nothing at all to ensure a safe birth. On the contrary, for most modern women there is a great deal of mental and emotional preparation that needs to be done before birthing alone is a safe option. As I mention above, most women will find it necessary to do a certain amount of "deprogramming" themselves of society's influence on their attitudes about birth. Each individual woman will have to overcome her own individual fears based on her own experiences as well. Ironically, some women assert that their reason for hiring a birth attendant is that "preparing so well for birth takes too much effort," or is "just not possible," while at the same time insisting that hiring an attendant due to this lack of will or ability is somehow safer.

On the other hand, it's important to keep in mind that all loving parents do all they can with the information they have, and it is always a tragedy to suffer a complicated birth or the death or disfigurement of a child. One should no more blame unassisted birthers who miss the one rare fatal problem that affects their child than one should blame a woman for choosing an obstetrician who pressures her into an unnecessary C-section or a midwife that transports too late. Without blaming the victims, I want to help individual parents make an informed choice of where all the "what ifs" end. It's neither safe nor responsible to close one's eyes to possible tragedies and select a birth attendant as though it was a game of pin-the-tail-on-the-donkey.

Midwives miss problems that parents find. Doctors find problems that midwives miss. It's a circle. A spinal tap may actually reveal more about a child's health than a simple Apgar score, but everyone agrees that spinal taps are so much more dangerous that they should be reserved only for certain emergencies. It's all a matter of balance. As I've said, believing that one's chosen assistant will catch all the problems is just as dangerous as administering a whole host of tests. If having the only available assistant is more of a danger than not having one, then by all means parents should be encouraged to choose the lesser of two evils. Hopefully they will do so with as much helpful information as humanly possible. It's a shame that women are cut off from many resources of information because of malpractice law, but that doesn't mean women shouldn't be looking to possess this wisdom for themselves.

Unassisted childbirth may be the safest option for many more women than actually know it. Making an informed choice means being informed of the risks of attended birth. Some very excellent midwives and a few obstetricians have a number of positives to weigh against any possible negatives of having an assistant. I expect thinking people to weigh the risks against the benefits of any birth practice and choose what they believe is safest. The reality is, though, for most people the idea that attended birth is automatically safer is a foregone conclusion. Making such an assumption, however, can be far more dangerous than unassisted birth all by itself. If anything I'm saying is truly radically different from mainstream opinion, it is that women and their partners are fully capable of making these choices for themselves. In fact, the families who are potential consumers of birth assistance are the only rightful owners of these decisions and the responsibility that follows.

# 11

## *What can and should be done to help all women have safe, satisfying, joyous births?*

Nancy Wainer Cohen also said, "Believe in the safety of birth. Birth is not dangerous. Hang out with women who have a healthy attitude about birth. Take classes given by independent instructors. Remember that any intervention may confuse the body, and adversely affect the mother, the baby and the birth. Eat well and focus on prevention" (16). My message could hardly be more simply put!

When Nancy suggests taking classes she touches on an essential traditional role that modern midwives and childbirth educators currently fill—as a neutral 3rd party to suggest things that might help during labor. That is the ancient role of the experienced wise woman. It's a beautiful, endearing role, which is why I fully support a woman's right to hire midwives and the like if she so chooses. It's also why I warn women of the dangers of choosing the wrong birth attendant. As I have shown, many women aren't actually benefited by having a third party present in their house to fulfill this ancient role for them, but the information and support should still be readily available and acceptable for them.

Women also ought to be able to have such "wise women's" experience and an unassisted birth, even if they birth that way by accident. I mentioned earlier that many people first find out about the unassisted birth option while searching for less financially straining options than traditionally assisted birth. This must surely call into question the morality of charging a woman for a safe birth. All women deserve the safest, most pleasurable births available to them! So what can be done?

# Where can/do women get their information right now?

Western women get the bulk of their pregnancy and birth information from primary care physicians and obstetricians whose emphasis is on pathology—in other words, the things that can "go wrong" in pregnancy and birth. Many of these physicians see "informed" women as problematic, because they ask too many questions and make too many demands to fit easily into the assisted birth system. Professionals who attend births often prefer an uninformed mother. This seems to rest on the grounds that women don't need the information because the birth professionals have it. On some level, that exclusive information may be those professionals' only rationale for charging money for their services, so they cannot give it away. There is also often an assumption that the average woman is too ignorant or too incompetent to manage her own birth experience. This attitude asserts that women cannot birth alone, so giving them information only makes them difficult "patients." These professionals surely know on some level that the more information a woman has, the less likely she will be to choose their particular brand of assisted birth.

This is true of many midwives as well as physicians. Some midwives claim to favor women's empowerment, but when a woman asserts herself on the basis of accurate and empowering information, some of the very same midwives feel threatened and sometimes even become openly abusive and coercive. For the average woman then, the only way to find helpful alternative birth information is to read a lot of books and periodicals. It would be impossible to list all of the materials that have ever been helpful to unassisted birthers, especially considering the fact that much of what individuals find helpful is dependent on their individual needs, but here is an attempt to give a brief start:

Childbirth Without Fear by Grantly Dick Read
Unassisted Childbirth by Laura Kaplan Shanley
Unassisted Homebirth: an Act of Love by Lynn Griesemer
Pleasurable Husband Wife Childbirth by Marylin Moran
Heart And Hands by Elizabeth Davis
Emergency Childbirth by Gregory White
Special Delivery by Rahima Baldwin Dancy
Birth Without Violence by Frederick Leboyer
Spiritual Midwifery by Ina Mae Gaskin
Compleat Mother magazine
Mothering magazine
Letters From Home newsletter
New Nativity II newsletter

Thankfully, today there is also a wealth of information literally available at the very fingertips of anyone with a modem. Families planning unassisted birth can find support, resources, and information on email loops and lists like the Unassisted Childbirth list. In addition, there are a number of web sites on the Internet devoted to providing information and support for unassisted birth. For instance:

Laura Shanley's Bornfree site:
**http://www.unassistedchildbirth.com**
Charity Gregson's Unassisted Childbirth site:
**http://www.kjv.com/family/homebirth.hts**
Charity's bulletin board:
**http://www.kjv.com/family/bboard/bboard.hts**
Lynn Griesemer's Unassisted Homebirth site:
**http://ourworld.compuserve.com/homepages/bgriesemer/**
Stephanie's Unassisted Childbirth page:
**http://www.geocities.com/Heartland/Flats/3995/unassisted.html**

Maggi's Birthing Spirit site:

**http://users.fastrans.net/burness/magg/birthing_spirit/**

Kristie's Bestfed site:

**http://www.bestfed.com/**

Kristie's Unassisted Childbirth email list information page:

**http://www.bestfed.com/childbirth/freebirth.htm**

Laurie's Thoughts On Childbirth site:

**http://members.home.net/lmommy/thoughts.html**

# Where else could women get their information about birth?

Laura Shanley once co-authored a newsletter whose subtitle was, "Restoring Our Faith In Birth." This is surely what she and many others who spread the word about the safety and beauty of childbirth that is not assisted by professionals are doing. With anecdotal stories of real women's confident, empowered, uplifting, happy, safe homebirths becoming more and more available, faith is truly spreading. Increasingly, women are finding themselves in the same position I once did, expecting a child and thirsting for a better way. These honest, real life accounts are very satisfying. They fill the gap where the ancient tradition of women handing down generations of accumulated wisdom about the safety of birth and knowledge of how to handle common complications should be.

There is also the three-year-old (as of December 1999) network of women offering each other support on an internet community called the Unassisted Childbirth Email List (also known simply as the "UC list"), and more such email support lists are being created every day. A webpage of frequently asked questions and their answers is provided by the UC list, and moderators are busy compiling a list of archived conversations for future reference. Families planning unassisted birth like those on the UC list are asking and finding answers to questions like the following and more:

Why would anyone want to birth unassisted?

Can you choose an unassisted birth late into your pregnancy?

What are some good books/resources to check out?

How do you deal with a partner who has significantly different beliefs about birth?

How do you handle family and friends who are upset about your choice to birth unassisted?

Is unassisted birth legal?

How do you go about obtaining a birth certificate?

What do you do for prenatal care?

Do you need to monitor the baby's heartbeat and how?

What if you go into early labor?

What if you go past your due date?

What if labor is progressing slowly?

Are their ways to induce labor safely and naturally?

Do you need to check your dilation, station, and effacement and if so, how?

What do you do if you are having multiple birth?

What do you do if the baby is breech?

What do you do if you are Rh Negative?

What do you do if you have gestational diabetes?

What do you do if you were previously diagnosed with CPD?

What do you do if you test positive for Group B Strep?

What do you do if you have had a previous cesarean section?

What do you do if you have had a previous episiotomy?

How do you know if something is wrong during the pregnancy?

How do you know if something is wrong during labor?

What do you do for pain relief?

What supplies do you need for the birth?

Can you have unassisted water birth?

What do you do if you bleed bright red blood?

What do you do if your water breaks early?

What do you do to avoid infection?

What do you do if the cord comes out before the baby?

What do you do if you get sick?

What if the baby is born with the cord around its neck?

What do you do about newborn eye prophylaxis?

What do you do if the baby is not breathing after birth?

What do you do if the baby has excess mucous?

What do you do if you hemorrhage?

How do you know if you're losing too much blood?

What do you do if the baby or mother dies?

What are the legal ramifications if your baby dies?

What do you do about the mess after birth?

How do you cut the cord?

How do you know if you have retained part of the placenta?

Should you take your baby to a doctor soon after birth to be looked at?

What do you do about PKU and other newborn testing?

Do you need to vaccinate?

Do you need to circumcise?

Should you breastfeed and what are the benefits?

What does breastfeeding have to do with birth?

What do you do if you have trouble breastfeeding?

Shouldn't all parents be able to find their own answers to these important questions? Shouldn't all potential parents have such basic information before the birth of a child?

For various reasons, paid attendants usually cannot or refuse to fill the role of a mere friendly advisor. As I have mentioned before, paid attendants will simply lose business if they provide too much information. Some midwives may lose physician support and face malpractice liability if they move in this direction. Doctors may be influenced by their very narrow training to be distrustful of anything so low-tech as unhindered birth. Almost all birth professionals are at least limited by time constraints; meaning that they simply cannot give their clients all the information each would need to birth unassisted in the few hours of consultations allowed each month.

Yet, experienced birth attendants could easily share whatever wisdom their experience imparts, for free. It would be immoral for a midwife or doctor to keep life saving information from a woman who contacted her during pregnancy or labor with a question or concern. In addition, the role traditional childbirth education classes currently play need not vanish. Hopefully though, with more and more consumers of birth services becoming increasingly knowledgeable, the information presented in these classes will eventually become more comprehensive.

The customer is supposed to always be right, but for one reason or another very few consumers of birth services are being treated this way. It didn't take long before I came to realize that, perhaps in addition to the continuing efforts of those listed above, an organized form of volunteer help could be a valuable alternative source of information to professional assistants. Regular, run of the mill people could help other parents on the phone, down the street, in the living room, wherever individual families are most comfortable having them, I thought. My inspiration began to grow.

Perhaps interested and knowledgeable volunteers could hold monthly informational meetings—like free, unstructured classes in their homes. While thinking along these lines, I saw that a non-discriminatory "Birth League" of sorts should be formed—patterned similarly to the successful breastfeeding support group, La Leche League, but for unhindered birth. Such a volunteer effort, I guessed, could help all women attain the safest, most enjoyable births possible by providing basic, judgment-free information about how the body works during the conception, pregnancy, birth and postpartum processes, regardless of the family's choice of attendant. In general it would be very similar to what members do on the Unassisted Childbirth email list, only offering support offline as well as on, including directing families to important resources like the UC list.

It was my feeling that such a "Birth League" could easily prove preferable to professional instruction alone for many women and their families in the sense that, in such an environment, the birthing woman would more easily remain feeling like the responsible party through intentionally becoming more knowledgeable about birth herself, all without the power struggle inherent in paying a professional. I hoped that such a "Birth League" might also help provide the local support and community that established unassisted birthers desire. If any such volunteer group were to even become widely successful, then public education campaigns using TV, magazines, and radio could be started as well.

After doing some investigation I found out that author and champion of the husband/wife homebirth movement, the late Marylin Moran, had expressed nearly the exact same desire at the first national Husband/Wife Homebirth Conference in 1998 before her death. So, with the advisement of unassisted childbirth authors Laura Kaplan Shanley and Lynn Griesemer, I began work on this idea. With the support and aid of the UC list community, a few months and lots of hard work later I began the non-profit group Joyous Birth League International.

In March of 1999 I began self-publishing a quarterly list of contact information for members and updates letter for JBLI. Soon I'd placed the statement of philosophy and purpose for this brand new birth support group on my webpage, including an important form that people who wanted to get involved could fill out, for either providing or receiving support for joyous, informed, responsible, unhindered birth. JBLI began growing by leaps and bounds. In March of 2000, its membership consisted of over 140 families in over nine different countries and forty-six US states.

# Joyous Birth League International

*We, the members of JBLI, are actively drawing together as a network of families who agree with the following principles, and wish to provide and receive support from others in attaining safe, joyous, unhindered births. If you agree with the principles described below and are interested in benefiting from our free membership and receiving important quarterly updates*

*about JBLI, please visit our members page at*
**http://www.lauriemorgan.com/jbliform.html.**

## JBLI PHILOSOPHY:

- <u>When we say "natural childbirth," we mean **natural**!</u>

JBLI intends to boldly reclaim the term "natural childbirth" to describe, from this time on, the spontaneous courses of labor and birth as they occur when completely free from outside influences and interventions, or internal hindrances from the mother herself. The treatment of medical emergencies that occasionally occurs during Natural Childbirth should not be confused with assistance of Natural Childbirth itself, which is a separate spiritual, emotional, and physical process, not a medical event. In other words, when official JBLI documents say "natural childbirth," they are referring to physiological birth (characteristic of or appropriate to an organism's healthy or normal functioning) as opposed to any other popular definition of the term.

The basic philosophy of **Joyous Birth League International** is summarized in the following four statements:

- <u>Safety in childbearing isn't more important than satisfaction, the two are inseparable!</u>

I. The childbearing process—consisting of conception, pregnancy, birth, and the postpartum period—is one where physical, mental, emotional, spiritual, sensual, sexual, and social aspects are all vitally interdependent. Therefore, neither the safety nor the satisfaction that families experience during this process is more important than the other, and neither can be diminished or excluded from any birth without consequence.

- <u>Birth is an important but natural bodily function that proceeds best without outside interference, and for which women have all the necessary tools within themselves!</u>

II. To truly support a minimum level of safety, satisfaction, and sanctity in childbearing, the following principles must be understood, respected, and protected by all parties involved in any portion of the process:

1.  Natural Childbirth is, in and of itself, a safe, normal, healthy function of the female anatomy.

2.  Pregnant women and their babies carry all essential provisions necessary for Natural Childbirth within themselves.

3.  All births are irreplaceable and immeasurably important life events for all participants. All facets of childbearing are also fundamental parts of human life, and the events which transpire in conjunction with childbearing have a profound effect on the developing well-being of all members of the family as well as society as a whole.

4.  Babies are aware and feeling human beings from well before the time of birth.

5.  A mother and baby are necessarily and desirably interdependent during pregnancy, birth, and early childhood.

6.  Physically receiving one's own infant into one's own hands is an irreplaceable and immeasurably important life event for babies and their families.

7.  Childbearing is a personal process for all members of a family, involving unique, intimate choices, values, and beliefs.

8.  The familiar, safe, comfortable, and loving atmosphere unique to the birthing woman's own chosen family (mates, children, rela-

tives, friends, etc.) and surroundings (home, yard, beach, forest, etc.) are basic requirements for Natural Childbirth and for safety, satisfaction, and sanctity in childbearing in general.

9.  Childbearing is an integral facet of a woman's sexuality and is therefore intimate, and private in nature in a way that is unique to each individual.

• Birth is not an illness, and complications arise from treating it as such!

III. The vast majority of complications that occur simultaneously with Natural Childbirth are iatrogenic, that is, created externally, and most often by the circumstances of "assisted" birthing. "Assistance," "delivery," "care," "management," "treatment," and similar approaches to birth itself as rescue, or mere transport of the infant from within the womb to without—including the use of drugs, surgery, monitoring, and other common interventions—are incompatible with the very design of Natural Childbirth and are therefore detrimental to the process and participants, even in small amounts.

During the Natural Childbirth process, only a minority of families will simultaneously experience medical emergencies for which there exist treatments that are both morally and medically acceptable to them. Most often, medical care that is truly necessary and coinciding with childbirth could be, and most beneficially would be

1.  Supplied in the family's freely chosen environment if trained, equipped attendants and/or appropriate technology were available and legal; and

2.  Supplied in the least invasive and most individualized way possible as well, regardless of location. In other words, deviation from Natural Childbirth as defined above, should always be avoided as much as possible. Also, Natural Childbirth should, at the very least, serve as the example after which all unnatural birth environ-

ments are patterned, when they are deemed necessary by the family involved. Furthermore, any external interventions should be judged by their actual merits at all times, and no one method (allopathic medical care, for example) should simply be assumed to be beneficial or even benign without as much investigation into available options as is humanly possible in each circumstance.

- <u>Making childbirth decisions for themselves is the prerogative of every family, and can become like second nature to those that are given free access to relevant information!</u>

IV. Throughout the childbearing process, individual families are the most responsible for, deserving, and capable of making truly informed choices about their own care, and should always be supported to do so. In order to facilitate these rights, all families should be trusted, respected, and encouraged to make childbearing decisions for themselves, which requires being given unrestricted access to resources of information and ideas which may include, but are not limited to those such as

1. A basic understanding of how the female body Naturally works during all childbearing processes;

2. The mental, emotional and spiritual tools required by the mother to be able to birth completely alone if desired or required, and to do so safely and confidently;

3. An understanding of the difference between variations of normal and actual medical emergencies in childbearing and health in general;

4. A repertoire of basic safety measures;

5. A repertoire of basic comfort measures;

6.  A general understanding of the benefits of both popular and lesser-known birth practices and how each can enhance or diminish safety and satisfaction in labor and birth.

## JBLI PURPOSE:

JBLI has been created to bypass common obstacles to safety and satisfaction by providing childbearing women and their chosen families with uniquely respectful support and information based on the above principles. JBLI will strive to direct families to the sometimes hard-to-find resources that they desire, in order that they may give birth without unnecessary interference and hindrances. JBLI will also endeavor to provide its members with tools that encourage one-on-one support between families from all walks of life and all ranges of experience. While specific resources referred to by this network will come from many different backgrounds, the network itself will not discriminate against any person, so that the above resources are not artificially restricted for any reason.

This strictly volunteer effort includes, but shall not be limited to

1.  One-on-one and group contact between members, in person, over the phone, and via regular and electronic mail as facilitated by a quarterly updated and published Contact List;

2.  Group contact through all of the above media as well as through a. An official JBLI quarterly published Updates newsletter; b. Directories of internet web pages, email loops, bulletin boards and newsgroups that may be helpful to members but are not endorsed or sponsored by JBLI; and c. Live meetings (both JBLI endorsed events as well as informal member gatherings);

3.  Circulation of externally produced books, magazines, and newsletters—both informally between members and through JBLI sponsored libraries;

4. Commissioning, publishing and distributing JBLI developed materials;

5. Publishing and maintaining the JBLI website **http://www.jbli.org** and providing numerous online services.

6. Accepting tax deductible donations.

7. Promoting JBLI activities.

While our members will endeavor to provide the above, we have absolutely no intention of providing medical advice. At the same time, we are distinctly opposed to elevating the medical training, knowledge, or opinion of any outside individual or group above any individual's own intuition, instinct, divine guidance or basic human knowledge. Members and their families are encouraged by JBLI to take the information and ideas that work for them and leave the rest.

In order to protect our ability to nurture a vital network of diverse people who agree with the principles set forth by JBLI, our purpose is distinct. This singleness of purpose does not prevent interaction with, receiving support from and providing encouragement to other organizations with compatible purposes, but Joyous Birth League International will carefully guard against uniting exclusively with any other cause, however worthwhile that cause may be. Instead, JBLI encourages informed, responsible, and fearless choices in the related realms of family health, infant feeding, bodily integrity, education, guidance, and any other important familial concerns.

Thank you sincerely,

Laurie A. Morgan, Founder JBLI
Members@JBLI.org
**http://www.jbli.org**

# 12

## *Advice to women preparing for birth*

Is childbirth that is not assisted by professionals for you? Most of my audience has probably heard plenty of fear-laden encouragement to rely on outside assistance for their births before today. I, on the other hand, would like to heartily encourage women to take full responsibility for themselves and their baby's lives, doing whatever is necessary to feel like their very own birth expert, no matter where they choose to birth. It really is critical for all women to gain the knowledge and peace required to birth alone whether they actually choose to birth by themselves or with a hundred "professionals" in attendance.

On one of my web pages I used to offer those seeking a birth assistant the following advice: "I encourage women to ask themselves why they feel the need to have someone attend them if they do. It is important to clarify for yourself what another person's role would be before you can judge if each individual you interview will fit the bill. Any time that midwives or doctors insist on doing anything their client finds unwelcome, they are overstepping their bounds. If any person you interview to attend you in labor makes statements such as, 'I had to do (fill in the blank) to/for a laboring woman,' beware. An example might be a midwife that says she will let you labor alone, but she 'must' check dilation or fetal heart tones. As R.D. Laing said, "To allow is to exercise as much, if not more power, than to forbid" (17). These interventions will probably sound reasonable in the context in which they are presented, but be sure to seriously consider how invasive and inhibiting having that person insist on doing something unwanted to you while you are laboring would be."

I sincerely believe that when women begin asking themselves these questions many more will come to the conclusion that I have: unassisted birth is the right option for me. But first we must encourage women to ask. I won't kid anyone; if you are interested in unassisted birth you may have a lot of research and emotional work ahead of you, but you can do it! In addition to perusing the resources listed above, you can do what I did and use the doctors and midwives and childbirth educators in your area as resources. Ask them questions. Borrow and read their books. Pick their brains. Don't fear and revere them, they are only human like the rest of us! Above all, talk to and read publications by women who have given birth unassisted before themselves. Experienced unassisted birthers have the most accurate understanding of birth in its true, natural form, and they are uniquely aware of birth's miraculously transformative and healing potential.

## Conclusions

Childbirth is one of many normal facets of being female. Reliance on outside assistance in labor and birth would be understandable if the knowledge these people possessed about women's bodies were incomprehensible to the general public. But birth is a safe, healthy, basic function of our anatomy, not brain surgery. In reality birthing a baby is quite simple, and not the mystery so many people believe it is. The greatest thing that keeps unassisted homebirth from being the safest option for the majority of women is that individual women themselves have so little faith in their own bodies and abilities and therefore don't even begin to try to become informed enough to "do it" themselves.

It would be nice if women who desired company in labor could always labor with someone who would be "hands off" by default until the parents expressed an informed desire for help. In reality there are very few birth attendants who will willingly stand by and allow the odd woman to birth her own babies without getting involved in some way.

When one of those few people is not available to, or even desired by, any individual pregnant woman, she should not then feel pressured into accepting a second or third best scenario, and thus endangering her birth.

A few people in the position to counsel women about birth choices truly understand the capability inherent in the female body. Some wouldn't even discourage someone from an unassisted birth outright if that is what they wanted, but the same people very often would never recommend it either (this is a very common position among mid-wives). Some say that the wisdom to birth safely alone is too compli-cated or difficult to attain.

Actually, individual births get safer the simpler we make them. Some say that such an education would be too time-consuming for most or too cerebral for others. In reality, once you learn some basic principles, unassisted childbirth is no different from many new chal-lenges in life. They may seem intimidating at first, until a little infor-mation gives us the confidence we need. The fact that most people don't want to invest enough time and energy to ensure safe births is sad but absolutely true. Keep in mind, however that any claim that women shouldn't or can't birth their babies safely unassisted completely con-tradicts the idea that women can or should prepare for birth to any extent. As I have explained, birth is essentially unassisted, so if you don't trust unattended birth then you don't trust birth at all.

I can't answer for any one family what birth scenario they should feel most comfortable with, because the profoundly significant decision of whether or not to be professionally attended in birth is one that each family truly ought to make themselves. If families aren't even aware of the option of unassisted birth then they easily trade the dangers of uninformed unassisted birth for worse others. For one reason or another many birth assistants themselves think that assisted birth is best without question, and they make that choice for parents by keep-ing them in the dark.

Such an arrangement demands the question be asked, "What if unassisted birth is a family's safest option? Shouldn't true 'care' givers recommend it then? Or is it right to leave parents to find their best option by chance?" I hope this article goes just a short way to empower women and their loved ones to recognize when they are endangering their own births (by inviting unfit attendants) in an attempt to insure that nothing goes wrong. I also hope to help women recognize when unassisted birth might be their safest choice.

There is so much more to be said about unassisted childbirth. As I have noted, there are countless authors spreading their own important messages about the safety and normalcy of birth, just waiting for potential parents to listen. Sometimes women and their partners operate out of fear and lack of information, but eventually they find that truth is compelling. Our lives and those of our children are in our hands! We all need to take the initiative and research our options. Those women and their partners for whom homebirth that is not assisted by professionals is the right choice will continue searching and asking questions until they find what they need to know. My desire and aim is to ensure that it's not too late. Our part as a society of caring individuals, as childbirth educators, and birth assistants, is to make sure that all legitimate options are out there to be found and that the resources to birth safely are readily accessible and free for the taking to all.

# 13

## *The journal of my third pregnancy: a fresh approach*

Wed, 09 Sep 1998:

   I am feeling superb! No morning sickness this time around: Yay!!! The tiredness has even subsided a bit the past few days (maybe it was the vacation we took? Spent Labor Day weekend at a fancy resort [for free!—thank you Aunt Amy and uncle Mike!—that's enough to recharge me!!] in Northern Michigan, playing on the beach and eating out!) My clothes are just starting to get tight and I felt the baby move for the first time last Thursday! I was reclining and palpating my uterus (feels like a small grapefruit, just under my bellybutton, sometimes off to the right side a bit) and felt a distinct, "quit buggin' me" type of kick!! YAY!!! I love it.

I can even feel the outline of the baby when he's close to the front! Feels about three inches long butt to head and over an inch wide. Both times I felt him (or her) he was lying on his side. I haven't weighed myself at all but I think I must be pretty thin to feel the baby so early? Or could it be I'm just more "in tune" the third time around? Dunno. BTW, I was wrong about how far along I am when I [mentioned being twelve weeks along] before, I'm just starting the twelfth week today. I am still due mid March, I was right when I added those days up, I just skipped a period when I counted how many weeks since conception :^).

Thurs, 09 Oct 1998:

Still feeling terrific! I'm really starting to show. It's to the point where I need maternity clothes, and yet, all the ones I have are too large. How did this happen? It's very freeing and peaceful not to judge and measure this pregnancy by weighing myself, but if I were to check, I think that I would find I weigh less this time around than last time and that's the reason my clothes aren't fitting the rest of me even while I'm needing more room for tummy. Oh well, my mom is coming to visit next week (Yay!) and I have a cute maternity pattern; perhaps she will have time to help me sew a few new clothes. Other signs of progress: I felt the baby kick from the outside for the first time last week. Also, carrying Christiana (3 years old) yesterday I could feel the tendons in my abdomen stretch uncomfortably, so perhaps it's time to curb that.

My uterus is up to the top of my belly button, and baby is still mostly on my right side. I can still feel him/her really well but can no longer tell head from "tail", nor back from side. Still, it's really nice just to sit and connect with this little person and get familiar with his particular lines, bumps, and curves. I'm having delicious dreams about labor and birth lately too.

Thurs, 12 Nov 1998:

Another month has passed, and our baby continues to grow. My pregnancy is going really well! So well in fact, I hardly know I'm pregnant most of the time. Of course there's always this little one's constant, strong movement. I don't remember my other girls kicking so strong this early on (what am I now 5 months?). The other day I was leaning up against the half wall between our dining and family rooms and the baby kicked so hard against the wall it moved me bodily! Anyway, with two other little girls to take care of I focus less on the "easy" baby than I did the first two times, and it's making the time fly fast. It won't be very long that I get to take such advantage of this one's ease of care either, so I have to enjoy it while it lasts!

I've been trying to tell Angelica that there is a baby in my tummy, but she seems pretty oblivious. Christiana on the other hand, is very excited and loves to talk to and about the baby every day. I think it's cool that this little person is such a reality to her too, because I like having someone else to share my excitement with (besides John I mean, men just don't get into it as much as women do, do they?). I'm thinking that this companionship and focus of attention is one of the few things prenatal visits are really good for. I remember looking forward to my prenatals just for the attention the last two times anyway.

Thank God for providing me with loving attention in a way that doesn't undermine my confidence this time! Not that that would be an easy task for anyone to do to me at this point ;^), but still. I can't help but thinking that maybe God intended for first time mothers to be more focused on their babies, instead of on receiving outward attention. Who knows? In any case I'm immensely enjoying my freedom from the judgment and imposed worry that professional prenatal care can heap on a pregnant woman.

Physically I feel great too, as I have all along. For a few months there, pregnancy was draining a lot of my energy, but I was really just using that as an excuse. God showed me very recently that I had been allowing myself to step into a bad trap, by giving in to the feeling of tiredness. What I learned is that the more I procrastinate, the worse I feel, and then the less emotional energy I have to do the things I put off, while at the same time I end up having more things to do. So, I've made a new commitment to get up around the same time every morning from now on—no more "sleeping in" on weekends—and to obediently do the things God shows me to do as they come up.

I'm also trying to stop asking myself how I feel about every little thing (like "do I feel like doing the dishes now?" the answer is always no :^)), because that just causes me to focus on the negative. When I start getting that familiar old feeling of self pity now, I just ask God to show me some way I can be a blessing to others, which in turn gets me off my mind and then I start feeling good again.

Lots of people ask how many children John and I plan to have, and most are at least a little surprised when we tell them we have no plans of stopping anytime soon. I mean, I breastfeed ecologically, which makes me naturally infertile for approximately fourteen months after each birth, but after that we welcome any more children into our family as the blessings they truly are.

I'm really looking forward to being a mother of three! Yes, sometimes I think that the transition from two to three will be difficult, and yet I thought the same about going from one to two. I am keeping in mind how helpless I felt at first with a newborn and a two year old, and how eventually I figured out how to live, one challenge at a time. This gives me a boost of confidence and hope. I also feel much more at ease with the whole babyhood "thing" in general this time around, because I've dealt with it twice already. I can't believe how much I've learned about babies since conceiving Christiana four years ago.

As for the things I can't handle, well, I'll just have to lean on the Lord for strength. I've been in training for that for a while now :^). I'm almost getting good at it! We did get a minivan this summer, for which I am really thankful. Though it served us well, the little four-seater Festiva my mom gave us four years ago was almost broke-down and just didn't cut it anymore, even with just two kids. As it turns out, the timing was excellent. We finally decided to go for it and then just a month later we conceived!

Fri, 11 Dec 1998:

Well, actually it's Fri, 18th. I really had intended to update this journal last week! The thing is, I just couldn't think of much to say. The most notable thing I'm experiencing with this pregnancy is time flying by :^). It really doesn't seem like it's been longer than a week since the last time I updated this journal. So what's new? We're into the "tickle mamma" phase of pregnancy now, where this little one's extremities can and frequently do reach over and poke into that hyper ticklish spot just between the ribs and hip bones on my sides.

Every now and then, when I get tired of being "surprise attacked" from the inside I'll hold my elbows in tight, but not too often because I figure it must be important for baby to stretch out. Even with this new development, my aunt Nan commented that you can't tell I'm pregnant from behind. I checked with a mirror and sure enough, (though I can tell my rear is a little wider) my tummy is all sticking forward and not visibly sideways at all.

The other day this little one buried himself deep into my pelvis, it was a very strange feeling much like early labor. I kept feeling hands and feet swirling around the top of my uterus too, so he must have been butt/back down. I'm amazed at how much more aware I am this time around of my little one's positioning. As noted above, there was a period where I couldn't tell head from rear, but now I can tell where the head is because of the dip at the neck, and usually I have a tender spot right where the shoulder is. Perhaps that's because it's pointy?

The girls still want to be in my lap a lot, but it's getting more and more uncomfortable. Not that I'm so big yet or anything, just that having pointy little baby parts poking into bony little kid parts with my flesh in between hurts! I can remember being bony as a kid and my family would all complain when I sat in their laps and such. So now I guess my kids are paying me back :^). They can't seem to just use their hands to climb onto me, they have to use an elbow or a knee as a grappling hook.

All in all I feel really wonderful, which is precisely what I expect. I had a day long bout with the flu on my anniversary (Thanksgiving day this year), but other than that and an increased desire for sleep (hey who couldn't use some extra sleep??) I feel awesome. I am really looking forward to this birth too, in a peaceful, happy way. It's almost strange not to be filled with anxiety and concerns—that just isn't very common these days—but this is the way pregnancy should be! All joy and excitement for the new member of the family. I've got more to fear from driving on the highway than I do from giving birth, and yet the messages this society sends out are directly opposite from that. Wish I had an "emoticon" for thumbing my nose :^)!

Tues, 19 Jan 1999:

My sincerest apologies to those of you who are trying to follow along with my pregnancy updates at regular intervals! I'm sure I'm not the only one who got a little (more) behind over the holidays, but I still feel a twinge of sadness over putting this off :^). I'm starting to get the feeling that many things I have planned will "never" get done, what with the baby's expected arrival so near. For instance, I feel a sudden sense of urgency to finally go get the haircut I've planned for over half a year and just never got around to (nothing drastic, just the same old thing only shorter).

When will be the next time that I can have John watch the kids for that length of time once the baby is born?? Don't get me wrong, I could easily nurse a newborn while getting a haircut—breastfed babies are so convenient that way—but I'm picturing hair falling in his/her eyes. I've already decided that me and this baby are going to see the new Star Wars movie by ourselves when it (the movie) comes out too. I have very fond memories of Christiana sleeping through movies until about nine months of age. Gotta take advantage of that ease of care while I can!

Well, I thought I didn't have much to write about, but I guess I was wrong :^). It's just that I don't have the litany of medical concerns that most women at this stage of pregnancy are dealing with, and I am at peace. I've been thinking that it may be difficult to write up this little one's birth story when the time comes, because it will be so simple! "I had some contractions, baby came out, we all celebrated, the end!" I already feel this amazing body preparing for birth. My "braxton hicks" contractions are strong and frequent, taking my breath away and requiring a bit of concentration just like they did at the end of my last two pregnancies.

I also feel tiny little twinges in my cervical area. I'm not sure what it is, but I remember this sensation from my last pregnancies too—this is so fun! My imagination says it feels like baby fingernails poking me, but probably it's just a little early effacing or cervical stretching. What-ever it is, it's normal for me at this stage.

The baby has been head-down for over a month now too, with his/her feet usually tickling my right side and butt under my left ribs. Sometimes s/he turns around on his/her head and the kicks are on the other side, but only for a few hours and then it's back to the same old position (which coincidentally is the same position that both girls stayed in during the last months, with the small exception of their favorite foot rest being my ribs rather than my side). This consistency makes it really easy for me to visualize the baby, which I love to do.

I don't know how early the "nesting" urge is supposed to kick in, but I've been super productive around the house lately too. This week-end I got three drawers, the kitchen counter top, a cabinet, and the hall closet all cleaned out and organized, plus the whole house cleaned top to bottom (I mean crayon washed off walls and all!!). On top of that I've been spending more time nursing and nurturing Angelica, who is cutting some new teeth! So, if I don't get around to updating my jour-nal as often you know why now. Until next month…

Tues, 16 Feb 1999:

Whoa! I'm running out of room for my belly in photos! Guess the baby better come soon :^). I didn't think it looked much different from December to January, but there's no denying the change this time. Speaking of my perceptions of myself, I sure don't feel eight months pregnant. Other than this belly, my body hasn't changed much at all. I haven't checked, but I'm pretty sure I haven't gained much extra weight this time around. I attribute that to a higher self esteem, and extra work! With two kids to care for this time I hardly ever sit down for more than a few minutes at a time. Plus, my butt has surely benefited from moving into a home with stairs :^). I continue to feel great. My family had stuffy noses last week and I self pity-ed myself into a sore throat, but once I was able to recognize the root of those feelings and express my needs I felt much better. To think, all it took was telling my husband that I felt crappy, instead of stuffing it inside and feeling resentful. I'd rather have a backrub than a pity party any day!

We are all looking very forward to meeting this new little person "outside" of me. It's hard to believe that someone who is already so much a part of my life is going to be even more so in a matter of weeks. Meeting this new little person is the most exciting prospect to me right now. Who is this special person? How could God create three individuals so unique from just my husband and I? Is this the baby Johnny I've thought might come twice in the past four years? Or is it another wonderful person who just doesn't have a name as of yet?

Besides thoughts of the baby I've been having wonderful, warm, easy birthing dreams quite regularly. I think this is a very good sign, as it shows where my subconscious is focused. After Angelica's, it's difficult for me to believe that any birth could be more empowering and "mind blowingly beautiful" as I put it just weeks after, but how can it not be awesome this time? A good friend of mine still weeps at the thought of her daughter's birth, so incredible was the whole experience. I think we should all be so lucky!

Thurs, 11 Mar 1999:

I was running out of room for my belly in [pictures I took of it] last month and this month I'm running out of things to say :^). It's hard for me to believe, but this pregnancy is almost over! You won't be able to help but notice that I finally took a photo of me and my belly [above]. I've wanted to do that all along, but taking self portraits with two kids under three years old "helping" isn't easy. Anyway, glad I was able to get that shot before the baby came. I'm really happy with it! I've never felt as beautiful as I have during this pregnancy and I think it shows. Believe me, that's no accident either! My experience two years ago with the birth of Angelica has been more dramatically life changing than I ever could have imagined. I sincerely believe that God has used that miraculous moment as a springboard in my life to build my character, increase my faith, endow me with an all encompassing sense of peace and joy, and—not the least of which—bring an amazing, beautiful new love into my life!

Angelica is growing by leaps and bounds, as is her big sister. Whenever anyone expresses disbelief that John and I desire and welcome "even more" children into our lives, I think of how blessed and privileged I am to know and care for these two incredible people and wonder how anyone could not want to be more similarly blessed? I am so excited and humbled to be on the verge of meeting this newest member of our family face to face! I think the girls are excited too. Christiana has been thrilled about the baby from the moment I told her there was one growing in my tummy.

Angelica, on the other hand, has taken a bit longer to come to the appearance of understanding what is going on, but I think she finally does. Every now and then for the past few months she has demanded to, "see baby" which means I must uncover my belly so that she can lavish hugs and kisses and tickles on it. Christiana talks to the baby sweetly and "big sisterly," and likes to talk about how she'll hug and kiss "him" (she's always been sure it's a boy!) when "he" comes out. I had them both yell, "come see us!!" to my tummy the other day, I'm eager to meet my littlest love.

Well, as usual, that's more than I thought I had to say! Prayerfully, the next time I write here it will be an announcement! Thank you for coming along on this journey with me!

Sunday, 28 Mar 1999:

Announcing the birth of Cierra Lieghanne Morgan!

## Cierra's birth

I've started to notice recently that childbirth is sometimes referred to as an "ordinary miracle." The recent experience of my third daughter's birth really fits that description to a tee. It's only been three weeks since our little one's arrival, and yet I've already struggled with how to explain how beautifully simple, peaceful, and just...well...normal this birth was. At around my seventh month I wrote in my pregnancy journal, "I've been thinking that it may be difficult to write up this little one's birth story when the time comes, because it will be so simple!" I imagined it would all go something like this, "I had some contractions, baby came out, we all celebrated, the end!" I was so right!

My body had been preparing quite well for its third birthing day for a long time. I was still nursing my second daughter Angelica through this pregnancy, and so wasn't surprised at all to start having good, strong contractions at around four months, just as I had with my previous pregnancy. At around the end of seven months I also started having ticklish little twinges in my cervical area every few days that were probably the stretching and thinning of my womb's opening. Naturally, the contractions came more frequently and became stronger as time went on. In the evening of March 27th I was watching a movie with my family when I noticed that those nice, strong, pleasurable contractions were coming every ten minutes on the dot, so I assumed that the birth would be soon. During the night the contractions woke me with their intensity, which was something that I'd never experienced before. I knew that night that our baby would be born the next day, and assumed it would be that afternoon, as was my past pattern.

My husband and I woke up happy and excited but peaceful at around ten in the morning and spent some time alone together talking with a quiet excitement about the fact that our baby would soon be born. When I went to the bathroom I noticed some blood tinged mucous on the tissue, and danced with joy. "This is for real!" I thought happily—I had waited patiently the past twenty days since my estimated "due date". I was ravenously hungry and wanted a good meal before the upcoming "workout", so I drove to Burger King for my favorite morning treat: a breakfast sandwich and coffee. It was an unusually beautiful day that day—sunny and about sixty degrees—after having been cold, snowy, and rainy for months on end. I sang along with the cassette tape Angelica was born to the whole way. Burger King's drive-thru was closed, so I went to McDonalds instead. As wonderful as I was feeling, I still didn't want to have a contraction in the store and then deal with the employees calling 911 or something equally silly. Instead I had one contraction in my car in the drive-thru just before ordering, and another at home in our driveway.

I waved to the neighbors with a sense of secret delight as I carried my breakfast inside. Christiana and Angelica were still asleep and John was at his computer, so I ate breakfast alone and comfortable, smiling to myself in the sunshine coming through my kitchen window. Full and content, I went to work preparing my "nest." I swept the kitchen floor and cleared the table. I updated my webpage and sent an email to some good friends, letting them know I was in labor. I called my mom, and gave her the exciting news too. All the while I experienced the most wonderful sense of harmony with my body. It seemed as though my contractions only came when I was ready, or else I was just ready for each contraction as it came. Either way, they came irregularly.

Some were as close together as five minutes and others as far apart as half an hour, but there was no doubt in my mind that as soon as I relaxed completely, my baby would come gliding gently into the world.

When I started feeling pain in the lower part of my belly during contractions in certain positions, I went upstairs and set up our video camera. Then I laid a new shower curtain with a flannel sheet over it on my bedroom floor. I hadn't made any advance plans about where I would labor and whether I would try to capture it on video or not, this is just what I felt like doing at the time. As I labored I found that what felt good to do through one contraction rarely felt right during the next, so I experimented with different positions with each one. Sometimes I rocked on my hands and knees. Other times I danced, and still other times I swiveled my hips while massaging my lower belly. I was surprised to find standing and walking to be comfortable all this time, as being upright had been too intense when I labored with Angelica.

When I knelt through contractions more of the red-tinged mucous would come out, but with one of the last contractions I rode through while standing, my water shot out onto the floor with a pop. This was another new sensation for me, and I shouted about it to John, who was in another room, with delight. In between contractions I talked to the camera about my feelings and enjoyed the enthusiastic attention from my girls, who were awake by now. Christiana actually hopped around, saying, "The baby's coming! I'm so excited!!" John stayed in the adjacent room at his computer unless I wanted him during this time, and we occasionally called back and forth to one another as is usual for us.

During contractions I moaned and roared and hollered along with the intensity however I saw fit, which felt great. A couple of times I ordered the girls out of the room, and a few I demanded that John massage my back. I feel a little bad for being so brusque now, but it was good to be honest about those feelings at the time. Along with the sense of harmony I described above, I also had a clear and undeniable knowledge that I was emotionally resisting the birth. I literally knew for hours that all I had to do was allow the birth to flow through me—relinquish control—and my baby would be born immediately, but for some reason I just wasn't mentally "ready" right away. I talked with John honestly about this and he was very encouraging. I said, "I've changed my mind. I don't want to do this anymore." "This" meaning giving birth. He reminded me that I help women get through the very same emotions all the time in my work on the Internet, and that I could definitely find it within myself now to submit to the birthing power too.

All at once I gathered up my courage and began pushing with each contraction. This felt indescribably wonderful! It also felt different from my other births. I didn't really conceptualize it until a few days later when talking about it to a friend, but the baby was coming out in the same position she had been in for months—head down and facing my right side. Even though she was moving easily and painlessly, the sensation was strange. I felt as though she might exit through my rectum, so I rolled around a bit, grasping my buttocks while trying to find a comfortable way to push. The funny thing is, I remember now having had a dream while I was pregnant where I birthed the baby while in a sort of "crab crawl" position. The concept of giving birth while on my hands, feet, and rump seemed humorous to me at the time of the dream, but with this pressure on my rear it just happened to be the posture I was intuitively drawn into.

Sitting in this odd position, I felt inside to find a head full of hair just a couple knuckles deep. I was thrilled: our baby was about to be born! John asked how much longer it would be and I told him not long and mentioned feeling the head, so he stayed with me. All this took just a contraction or two and suddenly I knew the actual birth was imminent. I said to John something along the lines of, "If you want to call the girls in to watch, this is about to happen." To which he replied, "What?" (He didn't hear me.) I gave a final push right then and she slid gently out onto the sheet. Johnny says he had his hand on her as she came out, but all I remember of that moment was thinking how tiny she looked. Later we decided she was likely about 8 and a half pounds, which is larger than our first daughter was, but smaller than our second. That original perception was probably just due to the fact that I'd never seen my own baby being born before. As she lay there freshly born, I was seeing her a lot further away from me than I'd seen either of my other two babies for the first time.

She was beautiful, flawless, and purple, and she lay peaceful between my knees on her left side. I realize now that the odd pressure I had been feeling must have been from her shoulders. She never turned on the way down like many babies do, and came straight out, still facing my right side. My bottom was a bit sore and stayed that way for an hour or two, but I didn't tear. It was absolutely awesome and deeply satisfying to hook my own hands under her tiny newborn arms and lift her to my own bare breast. Her skin felt deliciously warm and wet, and I savored every single second of that raw, genuine moment. At some point one of us called to the girls that their sister was "out", and they came right away to smother her with kisses and gentle caresses. As I said, my rear felt a little sore, so we arranged some pillows along the wall for me to lay against, and all the action disturbed her into crying a bit. I tickled her lips, but she wasn't ready to nurse yet, so we just talked to her and enjoyed her while John snapped some pictures.

Just that moment I noticed that the light on the video camera was off, so I asked John to check it. Sadly, the batteries (which I charged up the month before) had run out sometime while I was still in labor, so we missed taping another birth. I think John had been blocking the view inadvertently anyway, but it would have been nice to capture the sounds of birth and moments after anyway. Ah well…The time was 6:00 p.m. so we assume the birth occurred around 5:50. She started nursing within that first hour, which brought on some of the worst afterpains I've ever experienced. After about three of these, demanding more back massage, and two Tylenol, I remembered how good it felt to push with my contractions earlier, and tried it. Out slipped my placenta and immediately the afterpains were replaced by strong but painless contractions.

We left our newest little one attached to what had been her lifeline until it was completely limp and white. I knew that I didn't want to use one of those hard plastic cord clamps on my soft, tender, newborn baby, but John did want to tie the cord with something. So, just to be safe I'd boiled some new shoestrings along with my sewing scissors that morning, and when I finally needed to get up and pee, John tied and cut the cord. The soft string worked just fine, and was much, much nicer than a clamp. With a small squirt of breast milk now and then, the stump fell away on the fourth day after her birth, revealing the most beautiful bellybutton I've ever seen.

I knew my first two girls' names while they were still in the womb, but John and I had never agreed on a girl's name this time around. I wanted to name this child Sarah Anne, or Annaleigha Sarai if it turned out to be a girl, but John didn't like these. John liked Annistasia after my mom Annis, but that reminded me of the title of a movie we've never seen, so we continued to toss names back and forth for over nine months. I really hadn't wanted to have a baby without a name. When it came down to it, I felt very odd to be naming someone we'd already met, rather than meeting someone who already had a name. But we just couldn't agree on a girl's name yet when our little one arrived.

The night she had been born, Sunday March 28th 1999, I dreamt of the name Leighanne; a rearranged version of one of the names I had wanted to use. When I woke up in the morning I looked at her and it fit. I told John and he agreed, but he just liked it as a middle name, so we still needed to come up with a first name for her. That morning, while going back and forth with a few more names that all sounded ridiculous, we remembered the name Cierra. It was the only name we'd ever both liked, it sounded beautiful with Leighanne, and it fit her, so it stuck. Our third little blessing is now named Cierra Leighanne Morgan.

I felt wonderful, healthy and energized after Cierra's birth. John pampered me and encouraged me to take it easy, but I was stubborn and went right back to laundry and cleaning house anyway. My body knew better what I should be doing and a few days later I woke up feverish with chills and muscle aches. I'd felt this way for a little while both times my milk came in with my first girls, so I didn't think much of it at first, but five days later I felt the same and had to admit that I was sick. I also came down with an unexplainable pain in my left side that hurt so bad it left me unable to walk around.

On Friday my mom came to visit and help out for a while as planned, so I hunkered down and camped out on the couch with my little one skin to skin like I should have done in the first place. I spent some more days weepy, hurting, and tired, and even picked a big fight with John one night, but I also got the intense one-on-one time I needed with Cierra and by the end of the next week I'd recovered. I've made it a point since then not to do too much and just soak up every ray of joyous sunshine that emanates from this amazing being that I can. I haven't been disappointed! So that's it, the story of Cierra's birth. It wasn't a terrifying, degrading, painful experience like my first daughter's birth. It wasn't a dramatic, intense, life-changing experience like my second daughter's birth. It was just beautiful and powerful in its simplicity. It was normal. It was birth the way it should be: an ordinary miracle.

# *End notes*

1.  Laurie's Intact and Ant-circumcision Links,
    **http://members.home.net/lmommy/circ.html**

2.  Laurie's Vaccination and Immunization Information Links,
    **http://members.home.net/lmommy/vaccine2.html**

3.  Brenda C. Coleman/Associated Press, "Study suggests false hyper-
    tension leads to unnecessary Caesareans"
    **http://www.canoe.ca/Health9910/19_csection.html**

4.  Doris Haire, "Update on Obstetric Drugs and Procedures: Their
    Effects on Maternal and Infant Outcome" Birth Gazette, no. 13:1,
    1996

5.  **http://ourworld.compuserve.com/homepages/bgriesemer/**

6.  **http://ourworld.compuserve.com/homepages/bgriesemer/**
    **presspg.html**

7.  Karen Plomp's Birth Stories site, **http://www.geocities.com/**
    **Heartland/7269/**, Labor Of Love's Birth Stories page,
    **http://www.thelaboroflove.com/birthstories/index.shtml**, Par-
    ent's Place Birth Stories index, **http://www.parentsplace.com/**
    **genobject.cgi/readroom/midwife/stories.html**, Motherstuff's
    Birth Stories page, **http://motherstuff.com/html/**
    **midwife-stories.html**, Childbirth.org's Birth Stories pages,
    **http://www.childbirth.org/articles/stories/birth.html**,.

8.  "Maternal Mortality" Mothering, no.84, 1997 p.64

9.  New Nativity II. Newsletter by Val Nordstrom. Summer 1998

10. Gail Peterson, "Emotions are physical. They effect [sic] and impact our physical and psychological well-being." **http://www. parentsplace.com/genobject.cgi/laboroflove/miracle.html**, Julie Robotham, "Anxiety May Cause Low Birth Weights," **http://www.smh.com.au/news/9901/16/text/national13.html**

11. Michel Odent, "Why laboring women don't need 'support' Mothering," no. 80, 1996 p. 46

12. **http://www.parentsplace.com/genobject.cgi/laboroflove/ miracle.html**

13. "CNN Study: Drug reactions kill an estimated 100,000 a year," **http://cnn.com/HEALTH/9804/14/drug.reaction/index.html**

14. Quoted on page 49 of Mothering in the article, "The Epidural Express" no.82, 1997 p.46

15. **http://members.home.net/lmommy/childbirth.html**

16. Debbi Donovan, "Birth as We Enter the Millennium," **http://www.parentsplace.com/genobject.cgi/laboroflove/ milennium.html**

17. Mothering, no. 64, 1992, p. 22

# Bibliography

Compleat Mother magazine.

Dick Read, Grantly. Childbirth Without Fear.

Gaskin, Ina Mae. Spiritual Midwifery.

Goer, Henci. Obstetric Myths Versus Research Realities.

Kaplan Shanley, Laura. Letters From Home newsletter.

Kaplan Shanley, Laura. Unassisted Childbirth.

Kitzinger, Sheila. Home Birth and Other Alternatives to Hospital.

Leboyer, Frederick. Birth Without Violence.

Marjorie, Tew. Safer Childbirth?

Mendelsohn, Robert, M.D. Raising A Healthy Child In Spite Of Your Doctor.

Midwife Archives.
**http://www.fensende.com/Users/swnymph/Midwife/**

Moran, Marylin. Pleasurable Husband/Wife Childbirth.

Mothering magazine.

Nordstrom, Valerie. New Nativity II newsletter.

RxMed, Oxytocin.
**http://www.rxmed.com/monographs2/oxytocin.html**

RxMed, Prostaglandin.
**http://www.rxmed.com/monographs/prostin2.html**

Stewart, David, Ph.D. Five Standards For Safe Childbearing.

Weschler, Toni, M.P.H. Taking Charge Of Your Fertility.

White, Gregory M.D. Emergency Childbirth.

# About the Author

Laurie and daughters (L-R) Christiana, Cierra and Angelica

Laurie Annis Morgan is a wife, home maker, home educator and stay at home mother. Laurie finds her writing inspiration in the joy of her life experiences and the desire to provoke her readers to recognize the superior expertise of their own internal guidance for childbearing and other related issues such as infant nutrition, family health and child guidance.

Ms. Morgan's collection of over thirty self published articles has been enthusiastically welcomed by parents and homebirth proponents on the internet since November 1996. Her inspiring birth stories have been printed in several lay publications, and Laurie publishes a quarterly bulletin for the non-profit support group Joyous Birth League International (**http://www.jbli.org**), for families interested in unassisted childbirth.

Laurie resides in Sterling Heights, Michigan with her husband, John and their children, Christiana, Angelica, Cierra and their newest sibling expected to be born before winter 2001.

Visit Laurie on the web at:
**http://www.LaurieMorgan.com**
or write to:
LMommy@comcast.net

0-595-26546-4

Made in the USA
Las Vegas, NV
25 June 2024

91464626R00100